DEVELOPMENTS IN CENTRAL ASIA

India-Kyrgyzstan Relations

DEVELOPMENTS IN CENTRAL ASIA

India-Kyrgyzstan Relations

Editors

Bal Krishan Sharma

and

Nivedita Das Kundu

United Service Institution of India, New Delhi

in collaboration with

International Ataturk Alatoo University, Bishkek, Kyrgyzstan

PENTAGON PRESS

Developments in Central Asia: India-Kyrgyzstan Relations
Editors: Bal Krishan Sharma and Nivedita Das Kundu

First Published in 2017

ISBN 978-81-8274-929-0

Published by

PENTAGON PRESS
206, Peacock Lane, Shahpur Jat
New Delhi-110049
Phones: 011-64706243, 26491568
Telefax: 011-26490600
email: rajan@pentagonpress.in
website: www.pentagonpress.in

Printed at Aegean Offset Printers, Greater Noida

Contents

Foreword

This book is the outcome of a joint research conducted by the scholars from Center for Strategic Studies and Simulation (CS3), United Service Institution of India (USI) and International Ataturk Alatoo University (IAAU), Bishkek, Kyrgyzstan. The aim of this joint-research publication is to bring out both Indian and Kyrgyz perspectives in one collection. Therefore, the chapters in this book narrate various viewpoints, opportunities, concerns and challenges regarding Central Asian Republics in general, and Kyrgyzstan in particular. A key idea that has emerged from this volume is that India and the Central Asian Republics have similar approaches towards major international and regional issues. India may not be a key player in the region at the moment due to lack of direct access but in the coming years, India will be able to connect to the region through the North South Corridor and Chabahar-Zaranj-Delaram route, which will increase Indian economic links with Central Asian Republics. Accession to the Shanghai Cooperation Organsation will provide India with institutional mechanism to be more active in the region. This will also benefit the Central Asian Republics in areas like investments, information and communication technology, space, agriculture, healthcare, and small and medium scale industry. India's presence in the region is in accordance with 'multi-vector' foreign policy pursued by the Central Asian Republics, which allows them to avoid dependence on any particular country. Central Asian Republics follow 'cooperative balancing' in their major power relations in order to avoid tensions. If they can sustain such policies in the coming years, the region will benefit economically, culturally and scientifically.

On behalf of USI, I express my sincere gratitude to the scholars and academics from USI and IAAU for enthusiastically collaborating on this joint publication, and for providing their valuable inputs and penning down their precious thoughts and understanding on developments in Central Asia.

Lt. Gen. P.K. Singh (Retd.)
Director, United Service Institution of India,
New Delhi

Acknowledgement

Developments in Central Asia: India-Kyrgyzstan Relations is part of a joint research project between United Service Institution of India (USI) and International Ataturk Alatoo University (IAAU) under the Memorandum of Understanding (MOU) agreement signed by both the institutes. While working on this joint project, the authors from both India and Kyrgyzstan supported each other for collecting research material, providing information and inputs through discussions and conferences.

We sincerely thank director of USI, Lt Gen PK Singh, for his unwavering support and encouragement. We also take this opportunity to thank USI of India colleagues, who were always there with their supportive and cooperative attitude for successfully conducting this project.

We also take this opportunity to thank Prof. Ibrahim Konkak and Dr. Halim Nezihoglu from IAAU for conducting sincere research on the topic and for their cooperative approach. They shared some insightful and thought-provoking ideas in their chapters.

Last but not the least; we would like to take this opportunity to thank USI of India's administrative and academic staff of the Center for Strategic Studies and Simulation's (CS3) for their encouragement and help. It is entirely due to the whole-hearted cooperation and assistance by both, the Indian and Kyrgyz side, that this volume has taken the present shape.

Bal Krishan Sharma
Nivedita Das Kundu

Contributors

Nivedita Das Kundu, PhD in International Studies, is Senior Research Advisor with United Service Institution of India, New Delhi. Her research expertise focuses on geopolitics, geo-economics, foreign policy, multilateral organisations, border issues, migration and strategic dimensions of security. Dr. Nivedita has worked extensively on Silk Route and transport corridor issues and concerns. She has contributed widely and worked on her research expertise in India and abroad. She has authored and edited books, monographs and published research articles on her area of research.

Halim Nezihoglu, PhD, is head of the Department of International Relations and Vice-Rector at International Ataturk Alatoo University. His research interests center around national identity and ethnic relations in Central Asia and Turkey, relations between Turkey and Central Asian Republics, democratisation process in Central Asia and the Middle East and legacies of colonialism in the Middle East. He has several published articles in academic journals in Kyrgyzstan and in other Central Asian countries.

Bal Krishan Sharma, AVSM. SM** (Retd.), is the Deputy Director Research and Head of Centre for Strategic Studies and Simulation at United Service Institution (USI) of India, New Delhi. He specialises in Strategic Net Assessments, Scenario Building and Gaming. He conducts strategic games for the National Defence Collage, Higher Command Course of the Army, Navy and Air Force, and Academy of India Foreign Service, New Delhi. He has edited books and digital magazine for USI of India titled Strategic Perspective, and also written articles in Indian Foreign Journals on strategic affairs. He regularly delivers lectures at premium military and academic institutions in India and abroad. He regularly participates in international conferences as well.

Reena Pandey, IFS, served in various capacities in the Indian Missions in Brussels, Manila, Kathmandu, London and Istanbul. Her last posting was as Ambassador of India to Armenia and Georgia. She was the Advisor to the Federation of Indian Chambers of Commerce and Industry for a project in Turkey. She also served as a Consultant for Eurasia Division in the Ministry of External Affairs. She delivers lectures at premium institutions.

Ibrahim Koncak, PhD in Political Science, is Director of Silk Road Research Centre and Coordinator of Languages Teaching Department at International Ataturk Alatoo University. He received his BA degree in English and Russian Literature from World Languages faculty at Osh State University in 1999, did MA in International Relations, and PhD in Political Science. He has lectured in different universities in Kyrgyzstan for 17 years. His research area is Central Asia and Silk Roads.

Raj Kumar Sharma, PhD, is from the Centre for Russian and Central Asian Studies, Jawaharlal Nehru University, New Delhi. Currently, he is working as an Associate Fellow at the United Service Institution of India, New Delhi.

Abbreviations

ANSF	Afghan National Security Forces
AQIS	al-Qaeda in Indian Subcontinent
BRICS	Brazil, Russia, India, China and South Africa
CARs	Central Asian Republics
CASA	Central Asia South Asia
CIS	Commonwealth of Independent States
CPEC	China Pakistan Economic Corridor
CSTO	Collective Security Treaty Organisation
ECO	Economic Cooperation Organisation
EEU	Eurasian Economic Union
EU	European Union
ETIM	East Turkestan Islamic Movement
FATA	Federally Administered Tribal Areas
FTA	Free Trade Agreement
HDI	Human Development Index
IBSA	India, Brazil, South Africa
INSTC	International North South Corridor
IMU	Islamic Movement of Uzbekistan

IOM	International Organisation for Migration
IPI	Iran, Pakistan, India
IRPT	Islamic Renaissance Party of Tajikistan
ISI	Inter-Services Intelligence
ISIS	Islamic State of Iraq and Syria
ITEC	Indian Technical and Economic Cooperation
NATO	North Atlantic Treaty Organisation
NDN	Northern Distribution Network
NUG	National Unity Government
OIC	Organisation of Islamic Cooperation
QCG	Quadrilateral Coordination Group
SAARC	South Asian Association for Regional Cooperation
SCO	Shanghai Cooperation Organisation
TAPI	Turkmenistan–Afghanistan–Pakistan–India
TTP	Tehrik-i-Taliban Pakistan
UNHCR	United Nations High Commissioner for Refugees
UNSC	United Nations Security Council
USSR	Union of Soviet Socialist Republics
WMD	Weapon of Mass Destruction

Introduction
The Geopolitical Dynamics of Central Asia

Nivedita Das Kundu

Central Asia had historically been a zone of India's civilisational influence. In Soviet times, the Central Asian region was called *Sredniaia Azia* (Middle Asia). *Sredniaia Azia* includes Kyrgyzstan, Tajikistan, Turkmenistan, Uzbekistan and Kazakhstan. Western scholars mostly use the term 'Central Asia', while some Russians have not yet dropped the old term, 'Middle Asia.' Another term, 'Greater Central Asia', is of more or less recent coinage.[1] Recently, this term has been given more exact geopolitical specification and applied to the five former Soviet Republics, including Afghanistan.

In the early 20th century, Britain's geopolitical theorist Halford J. Mackinder called Central Asia the Asian 'Heartland' to highlight the region's geopolitical and geo-strategic importance in global politics. Mackinder opined that the one who would control this region would also control the whole world. Indeed, with the end of the Cold War and disintegration of the Soviet Union, Central Asian region has developed as an important geo-strategic region in world politics[2], even though some of the region's states suffered from localised conflicts as well as economic distress. Ethnic tensions continue in many of these states, making the region susceptible to instability and threatening its political and economic development.

The emergence of 15 independent states, as a result of the collapse of the Soviet Union in 1991, has offered new challenges and opportunities for India to broaden its bilateral and multilateral relationships with Central Asian states. Since the emergence of new Central Asian states, India has forged a strong political relationship with them. However, lack of easy connectivity has been an impediment for India's inroads into the region. However, in the changed situation, there was a need to shift its focus from the larger canvas of the Soviet Union to a smaller canvas to renew and build close ties with each of these five new Republics.

Throughout India's history, connectivity with Central Asia has been extremely important. Central Asia has been India's principal door to connect with Europe. These countries have deeply influenced India's history, culture and polity. Out of all of India's neighbouring regions, whether across land or maritime frontiers, it is with Central Asia that India has had the longest association and the most extensive people-to-people ties. Today, Central Asia gets significant priority under India's foreign policy. Historically embedded yet ongoing Indian ties until the end of the cold war continued peacefully with all the Central Asian states. Indian government developed increasingly intimate relationship with all five Central Asian states. Hence, movement of people, goods and ideas, including spiritual interaction, continued and added to this connectivity.

There are many factors working in India's advantage in Central Asia. India is viewed by Central Asian states as a benign power that does not pose any direct contemporary threat. There is a tremendous cultural attraction and liking that still exists and creates certain romance and mystique for the people of this region. India's 'soft power', which has captivated Central Asia in the past, has the potential to be a powerful tool of India's diplomacy in this region.[3] India's technical–economic assistance programmes like ITEC, particularly in areas of information technology, are seen as relevant and useful for Central Asian states.

India and Central Asian States want to be part of an extended trade network through the North–South transport corridor. International North-South Transport Corridor (INSTC) is a significant regional transport corridor project initiated by India, Iran and Russia. The INSTC project is an extremely promising project that is trying to revive the Silk Road connectivity, linking East with the West and the regional countries by rail, ship and by roadways for moving freight from South Asia through Central Asia, South Caucasus and Russia to Europe.[4] INSTC is expected to improve the linkages and increase the regional integration and improve trade and economic cooperation between India and the Central Asian states.

This book is the outcome of the joint research project between United Service Institution of India's (USI) scholars, along with the academics from the International Ataturk Alatoo University in Bishkek, Kyrgyzstan. India-Kyrgyzstan relations are going strong since the independence of Kyrgyzstan on 31st August, 1991. Within three years of its independence, India opened its resident Mission in Kyrgyzstan.[5]

The Silk Route that passed through Kyrgyzstan had served as cultural and commercial contact points between India and Central Asia. The Kyrgyz leaderships have been largely supportive of India's stand on cross border terrorism and related issues, and have welcomed the ongoing peace process. Kyrgyzstan also supports India's bid for permanent seat at UNSC and India's role in the Shanghai Cooperation Organisation (SCO).

The chapters written and compiled by the authors from both USI and IAAU tried to highlight India's and Kyrgyzstan's viewpoint on the "Development in Central Asia and India-Kyrgyzstan Relations". This volume has got the potential to provide a broad idea and clarity on this contemporary policy relevant topic under study. The chapters also tried to examine and debate various aspects, providing literary discourses and present dynamics of the region focusing on possible challenges. The chapters in this volume touch upon various policy objectives, providing insight into its reality. The theme of the chapters worked out with well-documented data based on primary source. The emphasis of the chapters contributed by the Indian experts provides India's perspective on the topic. The chapters written by experts from Kyrgyzstan cover various dimensions and share their views and perspective. All the authors share possible convergence and divergences of ideas too. Simultaneously, a critical assessment is also highlighted, and weak points are also discussed and identified by the authors in this volume.

END NOTES

1. Richard Pomfret, "The Economic Cooperation Organisation: Current Status and Future Prospects", *Europe-Asia Studies*, 49(4), July 1997, pp. 649–59.
2. Nandkumar T., "Celebrating 60 years of Indo-Russian ties", *Hindu*, June 12, 2007
3. Lena Jonson, *Vladimir Putin and Central Asia*, London: I.B. Taurus, 2004, pp. 103–12.
4. Kundu Das Nivedita, Murat Yulek & Humbatov Mahir, "Baku-Tbilisi-Kars Railroads: The Iron Ground For The Silk Road", *Sam Review*, Volume 13, September 2014, Center for Strategic Studies, Baku, Azerbaijan, pp.31-34

REFERENCES

Bakshi Jyotsna, ed. "Geopolitical Dynamics of India-Tajikistan Relations", Pentagon Press, 2013

Faultline of Conflict in Central Asia and the South Caucasus, RAND Document, RAND Publications, 2003. Also see Kavalski, 2007, p. 854.

Firdous T., "India and Central Asia", in M.A. Kaw and A.A. Banday eds. *Central Asia Introspection*, Crown Press, Srinagar, 2006, pp.321-322.

Kundu Das Nivedita, "Russia and its Near Abroad: Strategic Dynamics and Implications", Authors Press, Delhi, 2008

"India looking for energy supplies in Central Asia", 13 September 2006, available at http://www.asianews.it/index.php?art=7200&l=en.

"India-Central Asia Economic Relations", A Report of RIS/CII Seminar RIS-DP # 94/2005, May 2005 Kazakhstan Country analysis Brief, EIA, 2008

M.S. Roy, "India's Interest in Central Asia", *Strategic Analysis*, Vol.34, (12), March 2001, pp. 2273–89

Santhanam K, Dwivedi R. eds., India-Kyrgyz Relations: Perspective and Prospects, Anamaya Publishers 2006

Svante E. Cornell, "Security Threats and Challenges in Caucasus after 9/11", in Ariel Cohen ed., Eurasia in Balance: The US and the Regional Power Shift, Aldershot: Ashgae Publishing Ltd, 2005

Chapter 1

Nation Building and National Identity in Post-Soviet Central Asia

Halim Nezihoglu

Introduction

There is a vast literature on the concepts and discussions around nation building and nationhood, ethnic/national identities, ethno-politics and issues of nationalism in the world. The scholars who think and write on nation and nationalism have been classified according to their approaches such as 'primordialist', 'modernist', 'ethno-symbolist', 'constructivist', and so on. Although modern nations have primordial roots in history, their modern shapes, both in terms of form and content, are to a certain degree different from their prototypes. Each nation has its own historically constructed and socio-politically institutionalised mental image of nationhood and national sense. Generally, this unique imagination (see Anderson, 1983) in a country is enhanced by an official nation building or identity policy, specific to that country. So, nation-building and national identity formation processes in a country depend on elements of continuity on one side which has been shaped by a unique historical context, and on the other side, elements of change which refer to the current socio-political changes. The diversity in the approaches and conceptualisations at theoretical level in the study of nationalism is further expanded by the presence of different experiences and patterns with regard to varying historical-political contexts and unique evolutionary stages belonging to distinct ethno-national entities. National identity in a country has evolved into its current shape through unique historical experiences, within sui generis socio-political contexts, and in special cultural backgrounds and traditions. For instance, while national identity in a Middle Eastern country might have elements from their Ottoman past and post-Ottoman period on which British or French imperial policies played a key role, national identity in a Central Asian country has elements from their Soviet past. The question of national identity has risen to the surface in former Soviet republics after the independence, as the newly independent republics have become free and sovereign in pursuing their own national identity policies. This chapter points out nation-building process in Central Asia; and discusses national identity issue in the region in light of the historical context. Whether national identity model in the region is ethnic-based, civic-based, or a combination and synthesis of both, will also be clarified.

Historical Background of the Nation Building Process in Central Asia

Thinking in historical terms is crucial for the psychological dimension and the construction of an enduring national self which spans a period of time in history. Nations, however young, have a historical background. History shows that there is an ethno-national entity which is permanent through a long period of time and has a well-rooted essence. 'If the 'we' of the present time and future is the same 'we' as of all our past times, then what we have is a constant identity across all time. The *mankurt* concept in Chyngyz Aitmatov's novel, *The Day Lasts More Than a Hundred Years*, shows strong relationship between identity and memory. In the legend, the captive man named Djolaman forgets everything—his past, his culture, his mother and his own name even. National history and historical narrative is the memory of a nation. A nation cannot construct and keep its national identity without a national history. Every nation has its historical symbols and heroes. By knowing our history and our heroes (in history), we know ourselves. Their character reflects the national character. The way they are defined in national history defines how the members of a nation should be (Reicher & Hopkins, 2001).

All of the current Central Asian nations coexisted and intensely interacted with one another in the grand history of Central Asia. At times, they fought against foreigners outside the region together. There were two great names in the region, which included a variety of ethnic or tribal affiliations: Turks and Mongols. The word 'Turk' referred to a variety of kin groups speaking closed languages such as Kyrgyz, Kazakh, Kipchak, Uzbek, Turkmen, etc. These horse-breeding and highly mobile nomads of Eurasia and Inner Asia founded several khanates and empires together. As a result of climate conditions or wars, the region witnessed great migrations, transformations and political regrouping (Brower, 1997). It was difficult to draw clear-cut boundaries between Central Asian ethnic categorisations with their specific geographic locations in the long common history. Genghis Khan and his descendants predominated in the area from 13th to 15th century (Lowe, 2003). The evolution of systems of government and traditions of legitimisation which emerged in Mongol times remained in force until the 19th century. The process of differentiation was largely a political one, centered on the creation of tribal confederations and loyalty to strong leaders, most of them descending from Genghis Khan. In regions of Central Asia, power was not highly centralised, nor was it wielded entirely by the dynasty. Unlike European national kingdoms and successor nation-states, Central Asian political entities were organised as multi-ethnic states. The Khans retained their power neither through their central bureaucratic structures nor through the monopoly of force, but by their ability to win the loyalty of tribal chiefs to be able to balance the ethnic groups beneath them (Manz, 1994).

Central Asian ethno-tribal communities in the 19th century were loosely organised under the administration of the three khanates of Khiva, Bukhara and Kokand, unlike highly centralised and homogeneous national kingdoms of Europe (Schwartz, 1992). Russian occupation of Central Asia was realised step by step through 18th and 19th centuries; and total control was established in the region in late 19th and early 20th century (Saray, 1982; 1994; 1996; Allworth, 1994; Devlet, 1989). However, even in early the 20th century, resistance against the Russian domination did not totally disappear. In Central Asia, groups of mounted raiders (*Basmachi*) conducted a sporadic struggle against the Soviet authorities in and after 1916 for more than 10 years. Moreover, traditional social leaders of Central Asia declared the formation of the Muslim Provisional Government of Autonomous Turkistan in Kokand in November 1917. After the Bolsheviks consolidated their power, all remnants of such attempts and uprisings were totally eliminated during Stalin's period (Marshall, 2003; Broxup, 1983; Brower, 2003; Bergne, 2003).

Tsarist conquest of Central Asia started a period of massive change in the region. During the Tsarist period, intellectuals such as Nikolai Ilminskii played an important role in the creation of a new identity project for the non-Russian peoples of the Russian empire. Tsarist Russian education system, inspired by Ilminskii, forced non-Russians to learn Russian language (Tuna, 2002). The main purpose of the education was to give Central Asians a Russified identity that would simplify Russian domination in the region. These policies depended on a strategic mentality. If these peoples, who were struggling for their autonomy, could be assimilated into Russian community and culture, they would be receptive and loyal to the Russian authority. However, the unity among the Muslims of Russia and their linkages with those outside Russia would be a challenge against Tsarist Russian domination. So, the Russification project also included the change of alphabets and the exaggeration of differences between local languages of Central Asian peoples in order to eliminate cultural affinity in the region. However, some Tsarist educational policies, ironically, contributed to the first articulations of modern ethno-national identities in Central Asia.

Radical modernisation and transformation of traditional Central Asian ethno-tribal communities into clear-cut national units with definite national identities came during the Soviet demarcation of the region between 1924 and 1936. Until the Soviet period, within the wider context of Central Asian pre-modern regional political entities which were not nation-states, Central Asian communities, though they always had their own separate identity, was preeminently based on tribal/kinship rather than national (in modern sense) ties. Between 1924 and the mid-1930s, the designated nations of Central Asia were incorporated by the Soviets as separate republics into the Union of Soviet Socialist Republics (Vaidyanath, 1964). The Central Committee of the Russian Communist Party of the Bolsheviks held a session in Moscow on June 12, 1924 on an agenda: 'national and territorial delimitation of the republics in Central Asia (Turkestan, Bukhara, and Khorezm)'. In the same year, the following structures were formed in the region: 'Uzbek SSR (including the Tajik ASSR), Turkmen SSR, Kara-Kirghiz Autonomous oblast and Kara-Kalpak Autonomous oblast. The Kazakh districts were affiliated with the Kazakh SSR. This process gained its ultimate form by 1936 (Rahimov, 2007; Rahimov & Urazaeva, 2005). The Bolsheviks thought the division of Central Asia into national units would facilitate control by the center (Sabol, 1995). Lenin regarded the creation of national republics as a way of defusing potential national opposition to the Soviet state. He stressed the indigenisation of personnel in the political-administrative apparatus of the non-Russian regions, the autonomy (to a certain degree) in the institutional division of powers between Moscow and the regions, and also greater liberty for the use of indigenous languages (Dawisha & Parrott, 1994, pp. 9, 10).

The limited administrative and cultural autonomy given to the Central Asian republics during the 1920s was abolished by a wave of mass terror that intensified political centralisation during the phase of Stalin. The Russian officials of Stalinist era established carbon-copy administrative institutions in every republic and produced widespread cultural uniformity (Dawisha & Parrott, 1994, p. 11). Arrests during Stalin's "Great Purge" of the 1930s climbed to the millions including the social leaders and intellectuals of Central Asia (Fainsod, 1965; Goldman, 1996; Suny, 1988-1989).

Russians were regarded as the 'elder brother' and given a privileged and superior status over the other non-Russian nationalities (Gitelman, 1992). However, tough Stalinist policies did not continue in the same manner; especially during Brezhnev period, native cadres were privileged. In theory, Communism would eliminate all national differences in the USSR in order to create a homogenised single "Soviet Nation". This ideal was applied to a significant degree. However, "Homo-Sovieticus" to a certain degree meant assimilation of the other nations into the dominant Russian culture. The members of the growing Soviet elite regarded Russian language and culture as symbols of the privileged status. Many privileged Central Asians began to face difficulties in speaking their native languages (Medish, 1987). However, Sovietisation did not seek to erode all elements of national identity; instead, it sought to transform original identities into Soviet formation. In the Soviet-style national identity and narrative of history, anti-Soviet elements were downplayed or totally eliminated while 'unthreatening' folkloric elements were emphasised. In the Soviet discourse and narratives, central Asian ethno-national identities were purified from 'unpleasant' elements such as references to 'Turkistan' and commonalities with neighbouring Central Asian ethno-nations, which were perceived by the Soviet elite as threatening. Linguistic differences in Central Asia were given official status in written form by differentiated alphabets, and so became manifest (Igmen, 2004; Johnson, 2003).

Soviet period, on one side, put restraints on nationalist feeling in accordance with Marxist ideology; on the other side, it contributed to the development of national identities in keeping with demarcation strategy of Moscow in Central Asia. The creation of national republics in 1920s and 1930s with their own national elites, their own national name and national languages in previous 'Turkistan' created a suitable ground for the flourishing of modern nation-states in Central Asia. The Soviets created a form of ethno-federalism in which national republics represented titular nations; and they also supported the local elites of the titular nations in each republic (Bunce, 2005; Slezkine, 1994). Soviet system institutionalised nationality, and made nationality a main category in its classification of the Soviet population. Moreover, Soviet historians contributed to the fabrication of national histories within the framework of Soviet historiography, and so the new and modern nations were delimited on the basis of objective measures. Accordingly, Soviet linguists accentuated the differences between regional dialects in Central Asia and elevated them to the status of national languages (Phillips & James, 2001).

Soviet identity formation and nationalities policy seemed to have inconsistency, but indeed they stemmed from the same strategic rationality. On one side, the ruling elite and ideologues of the Soviet system tried to create a Soviet identity that would surpass local or ethnic identities in order to consolidate the Soviet entity by keeping different ethnic groups loyal to the Soviet political system. Nationality was secondary to Soviet citizenship or membership of the Communist Party. On the other side, they tried to eliminate supra-national identities such as Pan-Islamism or Pan-Turkism, which were regarded as political threats against the Soviet Union. For instance, the 10th Congress of the Communist Party of the USSR, held in 1921, condemned both Pan-Islamism and Pan-Turkism as deviations leading to bourgeois democratic nationalism (Schamiloglu, 2001). In order to hinder any region-wide integrative movement, as seen in early the 20th century in the form of Turkistan Autonomous Republic, emphasised nuances between Central Asian nations by the help of Soviet ethnologists on the basis of a pragmatic rationality.

As Graham Smith et al. (1996) stated, "While the center was engaged in institutional state-building and in creating all-union symbols of nationhood, one of the paradoxes of the Soviet empire was that it provided the social space for nation-building at the ethno-regional scale." (pp. 5, 6) Soviet supranational identity formation policies allowed a certain room for the expression of ethnic or national identities. For instance, the registration of citizens' ethnicity or nationality in official documents was commonplace and often obligatory in the Soviet Union. The internal passport was the main identity document for Soviet citizens. The fifth entry in these documents was nationality (Simonsen, 2005). Stalin gave politico-administrative status to certain ethno-national communities, and so ethno-national categories were rigidified. The recognition of national categories created newly imagined communities, reinforced by linguistic differentiation. "The division into categories was backed up by the intensive collection of the various oral literatures and the transcription of languages for teaching purposes, carried out by the Soviet ethnographers." (Dressler, 2002).

The idea of the nation began to appear in Jadid movement first—a cultural, educational and socio-political movement led by intelligentsia and traditional leaders of the Caucasus and Central Asia from the mid-19th century to 1930s. However, Jadid conception of nation referred to a region-wide supranational identity which was based on the idea of 'Turkistan'. Central Asian history was radically reinterpreted by the Soviet historians in a way leading to the emergence of a modern, nation-centered historiography that would be a base for national identities in the region (Ersanlý, 2002; Khalid, 2004). Soviet identity implied plurality in content but singleness in form. The passport performed the same function for all Soviet citizens, whatever their ethnic group is. As each national republic was multi-ethnic because of the demographic upheaval, it could be only Soviet identity that was able to unite all that plurality. Moscow wanted its citizens to identify themselves firstly with the Soviet Union, and secondly with their national republic but as part of the Soviet Union. Soviet period modernised and urbanised Central Asian agrarian or nomadic communities and created a 'high culture'. However, ethnic minorities who migrated to a republic did not see a necessity to integrate into the native society, learn the local language or identify with the titular nationality of the Republic, as they were comfortable with the Soviet identity (Elebaeva, Omuraliev & Abazov, 2000). Thus, under inclusive Soviet identity as a supranational identity, Soviet system institutionalised national identity as a fundamental aspect of personal and collective (Suny, 1993) but sub-Soviet identity, and defined Socialist Republics with clear-cut boundaries as prototypes for post-soviet nation-states. If pre-Soviet historical roots and Soviet transformation are not considered, modernist conceptualisation of nation fits Soviet creation of Central Asian ethno-national entities perfectly. According to this perspective, Central Asian nations are creations of the 20th century. In accordance with this modernist notion, people in the region were not identifying themselves on the basis of nation, at least in the modern sense as we perceive it today (Edgar, 2001). For long centuries in history, Central Asia was a region with a complex cultural composition and vaguely defined boundaries delineating political entities. None of those political entities were nation-based. Soviet project of reorganisation of Central Asia along national lines replaced traditional and loose political entities with clear-cut nation-based republics having titular nationalities (Esenova, 2002). Therefore, Soviet rule, paradoxically, created political and cultural framework for current national mapping and identities in Central Asia while attempting to create a supra-ethnic and supra-national Soviet space of multiculturalism (Beissinger, 1997).

The ruling elite after the independence has automatically turned to nationalism as the new ideology to justify the newly independent state and to fill the vacuum left by the fall of communism (see Gellner, 1995). Akçalý (2003) states that "The leaders of the five republics have adopted themselves to new conditions, and the existing bureaucratic institutions ensured smooth political transition. The elites became defenders of national independence, justifying their post-Soviet existence by national sovereignty and utilising national identity in order to legitimise their rule." (p.426). Current Central Asian republics as successors of the Soviet socialist republics are the most important base for modern national identities in these countries. Ethno-territorial units of the Soviet Union, as prototypes of nation-states, were viewed as national homelands 'owned' by their titular nationalities (Lapidus, 2002). Post-soviet nationalism has been a more or less unconscious continuation of Soviet habits towards the 'national question' (Fragner, 2001). Nation building process in terms of 'constructing and structuring a national identity using the power of the state', (Deutsch & Folt, 1966) and main building-blocks and institutions of nation building in Central Asia have been completed for the most part during the Soviet period. Post-soviet nation building policies of the Central Asian republics have sought to privilege the cultural and political leadership of the titular nations without alienating key minorities or jeopardising the integrity and stability of the countries, in accordance with the Soviet tradition and framework of the nation-building. However, this does not mean that post-Soviet period has not introduced any change and difference. Sovereignty in their own country and independence from the imperial master or 'elder brother' created a new context in which national history, national symbols and the other elements of national identity of the titular nations began to be emphasised more manifestly. Soviet symbols began to be replaced by national symbols. Thus, nation-building process, whose fundamental structure and groundwork had already been established during the Soviet period, began to be reinforced and consolidated after the independence.

Nation Building and National Identity in Post-Soviet Central Asia

National identity refers to those characteristics, symbols and institutions that make a human group a nation. In other words, it refers to historical-political, real or constructed, socio-cultural and psychological markers that make a nation distinguishable from other nations. Being a nation requires having a national identity. Without national identity, we cannot talk about a boundary marker that separates a mass as a nation from other human beings, and so we cannot talk about the presence of a nation (Nash, 1996). Smith (2001) defines national identity as 'the maintenance and continuous reproduction of the patterns of values, symbols, memories, myths and traditions that compose the distinctive heritage of nations, and the identifications of individuals with that particular heritage and those values, symbols, memories, myths and traditions'. Nation is a kind of large-scale community whose members feel social identity in terms of 'our understanding of who we are and of who other people are, and reciprocally, other people's understanding of themselves and of others (which includes us)' (Jenkins, 1996).

State has a central role in the construction of national identity. It is also the center of political competition over identity orientations. 'Nation' and 'state' constitute two sides of the same coin. The state is its formal and institutional side, and the nation is its human side (Liebich, 2003). Nation-state is, on one side, the product of nationalism and national identity, and on the other, the main source and base of national identity. Modern national identity is shaped by modern nation-state. Nation-states have emerged in recent centuries as modern entities. Modern states, in diversified patterns and degrees, have got involved in nation-building policies in order to consolidate national identity either in civic or ethnic terms, so as to make the cohesive nation feel strong loyalty towards the central government. Nation-building policies for the most part have depended on official national ideologies and/or programs. Official national ideologies, especially in newly independent nation-states, generally pursue to preserve and exaggerate the *sovereigns*, and in turn, assimilate or integrate the *subordinates* (Ozcan, 2005).

The formation of national identity, at least for the most part, depends on official national identity policy of a state. This includes the notion of citizenship in the constitution, official discourse and 'culture-speak', official history-writing, educational policies, language policies, cultural policies, references to national symbols in TV broadcasting, media releases, and in the public institutions, state-subsidized art, minority policies, and so forth. National identity or national feeling (perception) is constantly constituted by the nation-state's policies, institutions and its public sphere. Continual flagging, national map, national ceremonial days, national anthem, content of the educational textbooks, national historical figures and symbols, and almost everything like speeches, publications, newspapers, TV and radio programs, national currency, songs, products with the label 'Made In ...', referring to the terms or conception of nationality and nation-state are all reminders of national identity. They create an ever-reminded and commonly shared national imagination. The members of the nation are daily reminded of their national place in a world of nations. According to Billig (1995), this reminding is so familiar and continual that it is not consciously perceived as reminding. His concept of 'banal nationalism' is 'not a flag which is being consciously waved with fervent passion; it is the flag hanging unnoticed on the public building'. National identity can be found in the embodied habits of social life. Ways of talking about nationhood in daily life reflect national identity.

Conceptual and introductory paragraphs above set the stage for an analysis on nation-building and national identity in post-Soviet Central Asia. As a result of the disintegration of the Soviet Union in December 1991, a number of newly independent states emerged in the post-Soviet space. After the independence, there are some similarities in their nation or state-building policies with those adopted in many other post-colonial states because they also seek to remove some of the inherited colonial legacies. The titular nations of Central Asian republics have been in quest of a new national ideology since the fall of communism. They began to emphasise strongly their national values—religion, traditional ceremonies, national memorial days and national consciousness. Nation-state building has depended on the revival of national history, national language, national glory and pride; and the ruling elite adopted a new political-legal framework to this end by the adoption of national constitutions (Akçalý, 2003). Emphasis on the name, history and historical homeland of the titular nationalities became manifest in the national constitutions, which provided a special protection for (titular) national cultures. Soviet idols began to be replaced by national heroes such as Manas in Kyrgyzstan, Timur in Uzbekistan, Abai in Kazakhstan, Mahdumguly in Turkmenistan, and so on. Sovietised names of cities, streets, schools, factories etc. began to be replaced by the national counterparts. As they have their own language, territory and a political system, these countries can be considered modern nation-states. Russians living in the region were no more the dominant group but minority. They began to lose their former privileged status. Key posts in administrative bodies and vital sectors began to be held by the natives (e.g. Kazakhization, Uzbekization in cadres) in place of Russians (see Smith et al., 1996). While these countries are trying to get away from some legacies of the past, they seek to integrate with the world community and reorient toward the countries outside the former Soviet space.

A central aspect of overcoming this legacy is the revival of their authentic identity and history, and the creation of a national historiography that helps to consolidate the new national state. Revival of national history and language has lessened the effectiveness of ideological history and Russian language. History has been rewritten to get rid of the half-truths of the ideological history. In post-Soviet newly independent states, the revival of historical memory and national historiography required the regaining of self-esteem and the removal of inferiority complex imposed by the Soviet teaching. Historians, in this new period, are tasked by the ruling elites to claim the right of the titular nation of possessing a separate history. Without such a national history and as passive subjects of history, they would not be able to determine their own future. Post-Soviet states are in the process of searching for their 'lost' history in the pre-imperial era in order to state that they possess 'golden ages' and a new historical teaching that can be used to legitimise their newly independent states. New national heroes are drawn from golden eras as part of the revival of authentic history (Kuzio, 2002; Windschuttle, 2006). History textbooks are rewritten to give the students an ethno-nation-based conception of history which is required for the nation-building policy. They make a re-reading of their pre-Soviet history and revitalise some historical myths of the titular nations in each republic (Ersanlý, 2002).

The process of finding a new national ideology, which should take their cultural inheritance into consideration, is a complex and difficult process (Dawisha & Parrott, 1994). However, this process of change which includes revival of national identities has developed in a gradual way as it is restrained and checked by the Soviet formation. This is why post-Soviet transformation did not lead to widespread and long-lasting inter-ethnic conflicts in all the republics in spite of some conflicts (Luong, 2000). Soviet attitudes towards manifestations of national differences to a certain degree were liberal, pluralist and tolerant. Soviet system emphasised the right of nationalities to retain their distinctness. There were no rejections and total assimilation of non-Russian ethno-national cultures. Although ethnic Russians were overrepresented in the structures of power, there were no legal differences between Russians and non-Russians. Even though Russian language had a privileged status in several important fields, there was no rejection or elimination of non-Russian languages (Haugen, 2003). In the post-Soviet multi-ethnic context, a new national identity policy had to be forged between the demands of the titular groups for ethnic nationalism and the desire of the other minorities to maintain the civic nationalism that had been a hallmark of the Soviet identity (Huskey, 2003).

Some post-colonial nation-states in the Middle East or Africa, which emerged out of European colonial empires, were artificially created as nations and states completely by the initiatives of the imperialists. Some western scholars viewed the Central Asian nations in the same way—by considering them invented nations which were fabricated in the Tsarist Russian and Soviet periods by the works of Russian/Soviet ethnologists. Their modernist approach is not able to describe the whole of the real picture. Rather than modernist, ethno-symbolist approach can better define the historical reality of Central Asian nations. Before the Russian occupation of Central Asia or before Soviet demarcation of Central Asia into Socialist republics, there were no nation-states in the name of Kyrgyzstan, Kazakhstan or Uzbekistan with their current national borders. However, there were traditional khanates established by native peoples in the region and there were Kyrgyz, Kazakh, Uzbek, Turkmen and Tajik peoples speaking their own native languages. Because it was not an era of nationalism, traditional cementing forces (like tribalism, a charismatic leader leading a tribe or a religion) were dominant in the region. They were not political nations in current and modern sense. But this does not mean that they did not have ethno-national grounding. They have a long history which is full of national symbols and myths. They have existed as ethno-cultural nations before the modern ages. What more, they came together and established multi-ethnic khanates or great empires in the region. They cannot be considered similar to totally artificial nations of some post-colonial states (Weller, 2006).

Here, post-Soviet nation-state model should be specified with its general characteristics. Post-soviet conception of nationality is shaped by 'Soviet Ethnos Theory', which claims that nation is the highest stage of development of an ethnos. The leaders and scholars of Central Asia raised in the Soviet tradition are tending to primordialise the nation by describing ethnic identity as constant; historicising it by discovering its golden age and national heroes; and totalising their nation by defining it as homogeneous and collective (Abashin, 2006).

Central Asians' conception of nationality and ethnic identity is shaped by 'the Stalin-era divisions of society that divided the Soviet population into well over a hundred ethnic communities, which each enjoyed varying legal statuses based on size, history, economic capacity and location'. Five principle nationalities in Central Asia—Kazakhs, Kyrgyz, Tajiks, Turkmen and Uzbeks—deserved the status of 'Union Republic', and so received independence after the collapse of the union (Olcott, 2001). This process created a suitable ground for the immediate emergence of nation-states with their clear-cut boundaries and names without any problem in the post-Soviet period. The name of each newly independent state referred to its titular nation and was derived from their previous Soviet name. For instance, Kyrgyz Soviet Socialist Republic became the Kyrgyz Republic. The Kyrgyz, the titular nation of Kyrgyzstan, were native inhabitants of Kyrgyz homeland before the Russian occupation of the region. However, non-Kyrgyz ethnic groups, who are citizens of Kyrgyzstan today, are for the most part[1], immigrants who settled in the country during the Tsarist or Soviet period. The psychology of independence for the titular nations in the republics was shaped by this historical-political formation. They gained an independent state, in which they are the majority, with their own name on their own homeland. So, the independence and national self-determination (Neuberger, 2001) is perceived as fulfilled, as long as the titular nation is ruled by their own native leaders in their ancestral homeland. It was a historical opportunity for them for freedom from foreign government. National independence and national sovereignty were welcomed as these concepts imply the sovereignty of the titular nation in their country. The de-Russification of language, culture and education after the independence and cultural self-determination were understood in terms of the promotion of national language, the replacement of Russian names by native names, the revival of national history and the enhancement of national symbols. This process was not criticised by the non-titular ethnic groups and accepted as normal rights of the titular groups in their own ancestral homeland in accordance with the Soviet legacy.

Soviet Union had frozen nationalisms within the Soviet geography. Post-Soviet nationalisms were essentially the late 19th century forms of nationalism in which the 'one nation one state' principle predominated. Numerous ethnic identities were subsumed under the larger ones of titular nationalities of different republics. Post-soviet states continued this tradition. These states are conceived by their dominant elites and their titular nations as nation-states, as the states of and for particular ethno-nations (Goshulak, 2003). Both the ruling elites, who for the most part were the communist ruling elites of the former republics, and peoples have accepted the status quo (existing borders, state names, titular nationalities etc.) as a natural given. The assertion of 'ethnic' identity in state formation created new minorities and a need for defining majority identity or civic identity (Sengupta, 1997). Soviet and post-Soviet-type nationalism escaped the last stage of the transcendence of nationalism in the West from an ethnic-based exclusionary to a civic-based egalitarian project. According to Brubaker (1996), civic notion of nationhood is not likely to prevail in post-soviet Eurasia, given the 'pervasively institutionalised understandings of nationality as fundamentally ethno-cultural rather than political, as sharply distinct from citizenship, and as grounding claims to ownership of polities'. Thus, ethnic conception of nation-state is more dominant in post-Soviet states rather than civic notions of nationhood. In accordance with this conception, the ruling elite or the titular nation in, for instance, Uzbekistan, might hold the view that Uzbekistan preeminently belongs to the Uzbeks. Lack of civic national consciousness and ethnic or tribal solidarity supports the rise of such an ethnic conception of nationhood.

In addition to drawing on Soviet bureaucratic structures and institutions, the Central Asian states have underpinned their independence by elaborating nationalising policies and practices that seek to assert the hegemony of their respective titular nations. Despite formulations in the constitutions and other legislative acts guaranteeing the equality of all citizens, nationalising policies and practices are manifest in, *inter alia,* the iconography of the new regimes, the privileged status accorded to the local languages, newly revised histories and the exclusion of members of non-eponymous groups from the echelons of power. (Smith et al., 1996, p.139)

According to Commercio (2004), the term 'nationalisation', rather than 'nation-building', better explains what has happened in post-Soviet states. If we regard the term 'nation-building' as a process that transforms a traditional pre-modern state into a modern state by uniting the entire multi-ethnic population into an integrated nation on a shared national identity, the situation in these countries can be better defined by the term 'nationalisation'. Nationalisation refers to a project which aims to promote the political, economic, social and cultural preponderance of respective titular nationalities. Soviet system was highly centralised, hierarchical and authoritarian. The Russians, in such a system, had a special position as they were the most reliable and suitable group for the preservation and glorification of the Revolution, the official ideology and the regime. They were the 'first among equals'. After the disintegration of the Union, this first-among-equals system continued; and this time the Russians were replaced by the titular ethno-nation as the group having privileged status. So, the framework and defining character of the system and political mentality has not changed. During the

Soviet period, privileges were attributed to the Russians as loyal guardians of the communist ideology and the regime. In the newly independent states, in which nation-building policies replaced the communist ideology, an ideological vacuum in a centralised system is filled by tribal or ethno-national favouritism. Hierarchical, paternalistic and authoritarian tradition (see Charques, 1958; Nove, 1975) also had roots in the pre-Soviet history of the region. In the empires and khanates of the region, political authority was monopolised by a charismatic leader or a dominant tribe. If the leader was not followed by a charismatic son or brother after his death, the empire got disintegrated (Frye, 1996; Güngör, 1999). This long-lasting hierarchical tradition has had reflections for post-Soviet conception of ethnicity and nationhood in the region. Soviet system was also a centrally-commanded system. Politics, identity, social norms, ethnic perceptions and discourse—all were shaped by Moscow or the Communist Party. Indeed, the Soviet system favoured the titular ethno-national group in each national republic. In accordance with the principles of Soviet ethno-federalism, non-titular ethnic groups in the Soviet Socialist republics enjoyed cultural rights as individuals, but were not granted privileges that titular groups typically enjoyed (e.g. territorial autonomy, language protection) (Fumagalli, 2007). As post-Soviet pattern of national identity and nation building model in Central Asia have been shaped within the confines of the above-mentioned legacy, the primacy of the titular national communities over non-titular minorities is perceived as natural by the citizens of these countries.

However, the above-mentioned facts do not mean that there are no civic elements in national identity at societal or state level in the region. Titular peoples share some common civic conceptions together with non-titular citizens of the republics, such as territory, citizenship, political institutions and rights, and so on. They even share some cultural commonalities such as religion, language, traditions, and common ancestry with kin ethnic groups or a common Soviet culture and Russian language with all groups as remnants of the Soviet period. The slogan 'Kyrgyzstan, our common home', for instance, was also welcomed by the Kyrgyz people during

Akaev period. State policies contain civic and ethnic elements in varying degrees. In some policies, ethnic elements predominate and in some others, civic components are emphasised. Thus, nation-building policies on one side include changes that refer to the revival of the titular national identity, and on the other, continue some legacies of the Soviet past. What Central Asians live today can be described best by the term 'transition'. In transition periods, both—forces of continuity and change—are apparent. In the long-run, while forces of continuity are in a downward trend, those of change are on the rise. When individuals from different post-Soviet republics had met with each other in the initial years of the demise of the Union, they would have felt that they shared many things and many aspects of the same identity. But when the same persons meet later, they would realise that each country had gone its own way, and that they were becoming less alike (Dickinson, 2005).

Conclusion

Nation building and national identity formation or consolidation policies by the state elite in Central Asian republics have had contradictory directions since the independence. The contradictory nature of the policies can be viewed as a quest for a sensitive balance as well. However, although a sensitive balance has been maintained, emphasis on ethnic identity of the titular groups has prevailed over an inclusionary civic identity since the independence. Preeminence of ethnic conception of nation over civic conception at state level has a foothold in Central Asian societies. At societal level, primordial notion of ethnicity and nation with references to kinship and tribal-local identities is not only manifest in daily speeches but resides deep within the subconscious mind of the peoples as well. Consolidation of a civic inclusionary vision requires a radical mentality transformation and development of prerequisites of a democratic culture such as belief in civic equality and respect for diversity, and for the rights of others in these societies.

There is no a clear vision in Central Asia for a viable national identity model which would include alternative tendencies in the societies, incorporate the diversity of their citizens and satisfy the requirements of new trends in the globalising world such as pluralist democracy. Although the prominence and high visibility of ethnic tones in Central Asian national identity model is understandable and foreseeable in reference to the unique historical legacy—whether the maintenance of the status quo without any modification under the pressures of the global forces and trends will assure social cohesion and a well-grounded stability or not—is debatable. A full-fledged civic understanding of nation is a matter of democracy; and civic notion of equal citizenship requires an entrenched democratic culture, which is lacking in the post-Soviet space. Democracies are generally viewed today as better able than non-democratic regimes to handle the problems of multi-ethnicity (Riggs, 2002). Until recent decades, most states around the world tried to be nation-states in conventional model, in which the state was regarded as the possession of a dominant national group—which defined the state as the expression of its nationhood—and accordingly used the state to privilege its identity, history, culture, language, and so on. Those who did not belong to this dominant national group were subject to either assimilation or exclusion. This traditional model of nation-state began to be challenged both from within and from without in the recent decades. Instead, multicultural and pluralist democratic model of state has become a new trend among intellectual circles in the postmodern globe. In this model, the state must be seen as belonging equally to all citizens. Pluralist democratic state repudiates assimilation or exclusion of non-dominant minority groups. Citizens should have equal access to state institutions without hiding their ethno-cultural identity. Every minority group should be able to freely express their identity, history, culture and language; and these should be recognised and supported by the state in an equal way (Kymlicka, 2003). Generally, national consolidation in post-Soviet countries, with an emphasis on ethnic roots, produced a relatively weak civic inclusivity. The strength of a supra-ethnic framework and the degree of civic inclusivity within a national and legal order can be a decisive variable for keeping interethnic tension under control (Agadjanian, 2001).

As Mark S. Johnson (2003) stated, "... the region has been shaped by complex patterns of ethnic, cultural and religious syncretism. The only way forward would seem to be for the nations of the region to embrace this history as their own, to more openly and honestly explore their own shared forms of post-colonial hybridity and to accept that the principles of multilingualism, cultural pluralism, ethnic coexistence and regional cooperation hold the key to understanding both—their collective past and to shaping a more peaceful, economically stable and, possibly, more democratic common future." (p.33). B.E. Behar (1994) affirmed that independence has imposed a responsibility on Central Asian societies and their ruling or intellectual elite to choose a political belonging. This belonging depends on a rich historical plurality that it cannot be satisfactorily limited to one and exclusive ethnic identity. If it is emphasised in an exclusionary way, by excluding the other historical and cultural layers of a pluralist and multi-dimensional identity; and by decomposing a rich cultural background into a narrow identity, it would be inadequate for the maintenance of social cohesion. An all-inclusive new vision which has reference to the region-wide human, historical and geographical realities is needed for a pluralist democracy and a sustainable stability, rather than a narrow-minded, ethnocentric, sectarian, clannish and exclusive conception of nationalism emphasising differences rather than commonalities. Such inclusionary vision and concurrent policies depending on integrative dynamics, equal citizenship, a shared civic culture, cultural tolerance, meritocracy and impersonal rule of law would foster peaceful coexistence and social solidarity at domestic/ national level, and friendly relations and regional cooperation at regional/international level.

REFERENCES

Abashin, Sergei N. "Post-Soviet Nationalism, Ethnos Theory, and Constructivist Critique", *Anthropology &Archeology of Eurasia*, vol.44, no.4, Spring 2006, pp.58, 59.

Agadjanian, Alexander. "Revising Pandora's Gifts: Religious and National Identity in the Post-Soviet Societal Fabric", *Europe-Asia Studies*, vol.53, no.3, 2001, p.478.

Akçalý, Pýnar. "Nation-State Building in Central Asia: A Lost Case?", *Perspectives on Global Development and Technology,* vol.2, issue.3-4, 2003, pp.414-418.

Allworth, Edward. *130 Years of Russian Dominance: A Historical Overview,* (London: Duke University Press, 1994), pp.10-13.

Anderson, Benedict. *Imagined Communities Reflections on the Origin and Spread of Nationalism,* London and NY: Verso, 1991.

Behar, Bü°ra Ersanlý. "Baðýmsýzlýk Kimliði: Yeni Türk Cumhuriyetlerinde Kültürel/Siyasal Dönü°üm", *TürkiyeGünlüðü,* no.31, November-December 1994, pp.104-110.

Beissinger, Mark R. "State Building in the Shadow of an Empire-State: The Soviet Legacy in Post-Soviet Politics", in K. Dawisha and B. Parrott (eds.), *The End of Empire? The Transformation of the USSR in Comparative Perspective,* (New York and London: M. E. Sharpe, 1997), pp.157-185.

Bergne, Paul. "The Kokand Autonomy, 1917-18: Political Background, Aims and Reasons for Failure", in Tom

Everett-Heath (ed.), *Central Asia: Aspects of Transition,* (London and New York: Routledge Curzon, 2003), pp.30-42. Billig, Michael. *Banal Nationalism,* (London: SAGE Publications, 1995), p.8.

Brower, Daniel. "Islam and Ethnicity: Russian Colonial Policy in Turkestan", in Daniel R. Brower and Edward

J. Lazzerini (eds.), *Russia's Orient: Imperial Borderlands and Peoples, 1700-1917,* (Bloomington & Indianapolis: Indiana University Press, 1997), pp.131-151.

____, *Turkestan and the Fate of the Russian Empire,* (London: Routledge Curzon, 2003), pp.152-164.

Broxup, Marie. "The Basmachi", *Central Asian Survey,* vol.2, no.1, July 1983, pp.57-71.

Brubaker, Rogers. *Nationalism Reframed: Nationhood and the National Question in the New Europe,* (Cambridge: Cambridge University Press, 1996), p.105.

Bunce, Valerie. "The National Idea: Imperial Legacies and Post-Communist Pathways in Eastern Europe", *East European Politics & Societies,* vol.19, no.3, 2005, pp.426, 427.

Charques, Richard. *The Twilight of Imperial Russia,* (London: Essential Books, 1958), pp.12, 19.

Commercio, Michele E. *Exit and Voice in the Near Abroad: The Russian Minority in Kyrgyzstan, Kazakhstan, and Latvia,* Unpublished Ph.D. Dissertation, The University of Pennsylvania, UMI Number: 3137998, 2004, pp.29-32.

Dawisha, Karen and Bruce Parrott. *Russia and The New States of Eurasia: The Politics of Upheaval,* (Cambridge: Cambridge University Press, 1994), pp.88, 89.

Devlet, Nadir. *Cagdas Turk Dunyasi,* (Istanbul: Marmara Universitesi Yayinlari, 1989), pp.139-144.

Deutsch, Karl Wolfgang and William J. Folt (eds.), *Nation Building in Comparative Contexts,* New York: Atherton, 1966.

Dickinson, J.A. "Post-Soviet Identities in Formation: Looking Back to See Where We Are Now", *Nationalities Papers,* vol.33, no.3, September 2005, p.292.

Dressler, Wanda. "Conceptualising the Reconstruction of Identities in the Postcommunist Countries", *Diogenes,* no.194, vol.49/2, 2002, p.9.

Edgar, Andrienne L. "Identities, Communities, and Nations in Central Asia: A Historical Perspective", Presented in a Panel, *Central Asia and Russia: Responses to the 'War on Terrorism',* held at the University of California, Berkeley, October 29, 2001, pp.1,2. http://socrates.berkeley.edu/~iseees

Elebayeva, Ainura. Nurbek Omuraliev, Rafis Abazov. "The shifting Identities and Loyalties in Kyrgyzstan: the Evidence from the Field", *Nationalities Paper,* Vol.28, No: 2, 2000, p.345.

Ersanlý, Büºra. "History Textbooks as Reflections of the Political Self: Turkey (1930s and 1990s) and Uzbekistan (1990s)", *International Journal of Middle East Studies,* no.34, 2002, pp.338-347.

Esenova, Saulesh. "Soviet Nationality, Identity, and Ethnicity in Central Asia: Historic Narratives and Kazakh Ethnic Identity", *Journal of Muslim Minority Affairs,* vol.22, no.1, 2002, p.11.

Fainsod, Merle. *How Russia is Ruled,* (Massachusetts: Harward University Press, 1965), pp.421-430.

Fragner, Berg G. "Soviet Nationalism: An Ideological Legacy to the Independent Republics of Central Asia", in Willem Van Schendel and Erik J. Zurcher (eds.), *Identity Politics in Central Asia and the Muslim World: Nationalism, Ethnicity and Labour in the Twentieth Century,* (London and New York: I. B. Tauris Publishers, 2001), pp.19-22.

Frye, Richard N. *The Heritage of Central Asia,* (Princeton: Markus Wiener, 1996), pp.41-43.

Fumagalli, Matteo. "Framing Ethnic Minority Mobilisation in Central Asia: The Cases of Uzbeks in Kyrgyzstan and Tajikistan", *Europe-Asia Studies,* vol.59, no.4, June 2007, p.572.

Gellner, Ernest. "Nationalism in the Vacuum", in Alexander J. Motyl, (ed.), *Thinking Theoretically About Soviet Nationalities,* (New York: Colombia, 1995).

Gitelman, Zvi. "Development and Ethnicity in the Soviet Union", in Alexander J. Motyl, (ed.), *The Post-Soviet Nations: Perspectives on the Demise of the USSR,* (New York: Colombia University Press, 1992), p.225.

Goldman, Minton F. (ed.), *Global Studies: Russia, The Eurasian Republics, and Central/Eastern Europe,* (Connecticut: Dushkin/McGraw Hill, 1996), p.16.

Goshulak, Glenn. "Soviet and Post-Soviet: Challenges to the Study of Nation and State Building", *Ethnicities,* Vol.3, No.4, 2003, pp.494-498.

Güngör, Erol. *Tarihte Türkler,* (Ýstanbul: Ötüken, 1999), p.54.

Haugen, Arne. *The Establishment of National Republics in Soviet Central Asia,* (UK: Palgrave Macmillan, 2003), pp.229, 230.

Huskey, Eugene. "National Identity from Scratch: Defining Kyrgyzstan's Role in World Affairs", *Journal of Communist Studies and Transition Politics,* vol.19, no.3, 2003, p.114.

Igmen, Ali F. *Building Soviet Central Asia, 1920-1939: Kyrgyz Houses of Culture and Self-Fashioning Kyrgyzsness,* Unpublished Ph.D. Dissertation, The University of Washington, 2004, pp.88-145.

Jenkins, Richard. *Social Identity,* (London: Routledge, 1996), p.5.

Johnson, Mark S. "The Legacy of Russian and Soviet Education and the Shaping of Ethnic, Religious, and National Identities in Central Asia", in Stephen P. Heyneman and Alan De Young (eds.), *The Challenges of Education in Central Asia,* (Greenwich (Conn.): Information Age Publishing, 2003), pp.28-32.

Khalid, Adeeb. "Nation into History: The Origins of National Historiography in Central Asia", Stephane A. Dudoignon (ed.), *Devout Societies vs. Impious States: Transmitting Islamic Learning in Russia, Central Asia and China, through the Twentieth Century,* (Berlin: Klaus Schwarz Verlag, 2004), pp.127-145.

Kuzio, Taras. "History, Memory and Nation-Building in the Post-Soviet Colonial Space", *Nationalities Papers,* vol.30, no.2, 2002, pp.242-250.

Kymlicka, Will. "Multicultural States and Intercultural Citizens", *Theory and Research in Education,* vol.1, no.2, 2003, pp.149, 150.

Lapidus, Gail W. "Ethnicity and State-Building: Accommodating Ethnic Differences in Post-Soviet Eurasia", in Mark R. Beissinger and Crawford Young (eds.), *Beyond State Crisis? Postcolonial Africa and Post-Soviet Eurasia in Comparative Perspective,* (US: Woodrow Wilson Center Press, 2002), p.328.

Liebich, Andre. "Must Nations Become States?" *Nationalities Papers,* vol.31, no.4, December 2003, pp.454, 455.

Lowe, Robert. "Nation Building and Identity in the Kyrgyz Republic", in Tom Everett-Heath (ed.), *Central Asia: Aspects of Transition,* (London and New York: Routledge Curzon, 2003), pp.106-108.

Luong, Pauline Jones. Sources of Institutional Continuity: The Soviet Legacy in Central Asia", *Prepared for the delivery at the Annual Meeting of the American Political Science Association, Washington D.C.,* August 31-September 2, 2000, pp.5, 6.

Manz, Beatrice F. *Central Asia in Historical Perspective,* (Boulder and Oxford: Westview Press, 1994), pp.106-108.

Marshall, Alexander. "Turkfront: Frunze and the Development of Soviet Counter-Insurgency in Central Asia", in Tom Everett-Heath (ed.), *Central Asia: Aspects of Transition,* (London and New York: Routledge Curzon, 2003), pp.5-23.

Medish, Vadim. *The Soviet Union,* (New Jersey: Prentice Hall, 1987), pp.40-43.

Nash, Manning. "The Core Elements of Ethnicity", in John Hutchinson and Anthony Smith (eds.), *Ethnicity,* Oxford University Press, 1996, pp.24-27.

Neuberger, Benyamin. "National Self-Determination: A Theoretical Discussion", *Nationalities Papers,* vol.29, no.3, 2001, pp.391-418.

Nove, Alec. *Stalinism and After: The Road to Gorbachev,* (Winchester: Unwin Hyman Inc., 1975), pp.1-49. Olcott, Martha Brill. "Revisiting the Twelve Myths of Central Asia", *Carnegie Endowment for International Peace, Russian and Eurasian Program, Working Paper,* no.23, September 2001, p.14.

Ozcan, Ali Kemal. "Nationalism: Distilling The *Cultural* and The *Political*", *Nationalism and Ethnic Politics,* no.11, 2005, p.165.

Phillips, Andrew and Paul James. "National Identity Between Tradition and Reflexive Modernisation: The Contradictions of Central Asia", *National Identities,* vol.3, no.1, 2001, p.29.

Rahimov, Mirzohid. "From Soviet Republics to Independent Countries: Challenges of Transition in Central Asia", *Perspectives on Global Development and Technology,* vol.6, issues 1-3, 2007, pp.292-298.

Rahimov, Mirzohid and Galina Urazaeva. *Central Asian Nations and Border Issues,* Conflict Studies Research Centre Report, Central Asian Series, 05/10, March 2005, pp.1-16.

Reicher, Stephen and Nick Hopkins. *Self and Nation: Categorization, Contestation and Mobilization,* (London: SAGE Publications, 2001), pp.131-151.

Riggs, Fred W. "Globalization, Ethnic Diversity, and Nationalism: The Challenge for Democracies", *The Annals of the American Academy, AAPSS,* no.581, May 2002, pp.46, 47.

Sabol, Steven. "The Creation of Soviet Central Asia: The 1924 National Delimitation", *Central Asian Survey,* vol.14, no.2, 1995, pp.225, 226.

Saray, Mehmet. "The Russian Conquest of Central Asia", *Central Asian Survey,* vol.2, no.3, 1982, p.40.

____, "Russian Opinions and Policies on the Turks in the Tsarist and Soviet Periods", *Eurasian Studies,* vol.1, no.3, Fall-1994, pp.18-20.

____, *Yeni Turk Cumhuriyetleri Tarihi,* (Ankara: Turk Tarih Kurumu, 1996), pp.100-108.

Schamiloglu, Uli. "Ictihad or Millat? Reflections on Bukhara, Kazan, and the Legacy of Russian Orientalism", in Timur Kocaoglu (ed.), *Reform Movements and Revolutions in Turkistan: 1900–1924,* (US: SOTA, 2001), p.363.

Schwartz, Lee. "The Political Geography of Soviet Central Asia: Integrating the Central Asian Frontier", in Robert A. Lewis (ed.), *Geographic Perspectives on Soviet Central Asia,* (London and New York: Routledge, 1992), p.40 Sengupta, Anita. "Minorities and Nationalizing States in Central Asia", *International Studies,* 34, 3, 1997, pp.269-272.

Simonsen, Sven Gunnar. "Between Minority Rights and Civil Liberties: Russia's Discourse over 'Nationality' Registration and the Internal Passport", *Nationalities Papers,* vol. 33, no. 2, June 2005, p.211.

Slezkine, Yuri. "The USSR as a Communal Apartment, or How a Socialist State Promoted Ethnic Particularism", *Slavic Review,* no.53, Summer 1994, pp.413-452.

Smith, Anthony D. "Interpretations of National Identity", in A Dieckhoff and N. Gutierrez (eds.), *Modern Roots: Studies of National Identities,* (Hampshire: Ashgate Press, 2001), p.30.

Smith, Graham. Vivien Law. Andrew Wilson. Annette Bohr. and Edward Allworth. *Nation-Building in the Post-Soviet Borderlands: The Politics of National Identities,* (Cambridge: Cambridge University Press, 1996), pp.139-164.

Suny, Ronald Grigor. "Nationalist and Ethnic Unrest in the Soviet Union", *World Policy Journal,* 6, 1988-1989, pp.506, 507.

____, *Revenge of the Past: Nationalism, Revolution and Collapse of the Soviet Union,* (CA: Stanford University Press, 1993), pp.129, 130.

Tuna, Mustafa Ozgur. "Gaspirali v. Il'minskii: Two Identity Projects of the Muslims of the Russian Empire", *Nationalities Papers,* vol.30, no.2, 2002, pp.268-271.

Vaidyanath, R. "Select Russian Source Material on Soviet Nationalities Policy in Central Asia up to 1936", *International Studies,* vol.5, no.3, January 1964, pp.309, 310.

Weller, R. Charles. *Rethinking Kazakh and Central Asian Nationhood: A Challenge to Prevailing Western Views,* (Los Angeles: Asia Research Associates, 2006), www.ara-cahcrc.com,*pp.19*-24.

Windschuttle, Keith. "National Identity and the Corruption of History", *The New Criterion,* January 2006, pp.29-34.

Chapter 2

Terrorism in the Afghanistan-Pakistan (Af-Pak) Region and its Implications on Regional Security

Bal Krishan Sharma

Introduction

Geo-strategically, Af-Pak region and its neighbourhood form part of the same strategic space. The 'Old Silk Route' was a conduit of shared prosperity and cross-fertilization of faiths and civilisations between the Indian sub-continent Central Asia, West Asia and China. Many invasions into India came from Central Asia. In the present era, Af-Pak region, infamously known as the epicenter of international terrorism, has assumed the dimension of a strategic buffer to contain the rising tide of terrorism. At the same time, its landmass forms strategic bridge, connecting Eurasia with South Asia through an emerging network of trade and energy corridors. With the onset of conducive security environment in the region, prospects of making strategic corridors such as One Road One Belt, Maritime Silk Route, China-Pakistan Economic Corridor, International North-South Transport Corridor, Chabahar-Zaranj-Delaram-Central Asia, Turkmenistan-Afghanistan-Pakistan-India (TAPI), Iran-Pakistan-

India (IPI) and Central Asian South Asia (CASA)-1000 will brighten and promote peace and prosperity in the region. With the improvement in political environment, Afghanistan could get direct access to India via Wagah border, and Pakistan to Central Asia via Afghanistan. However, if we are unable to curb terrorism, the risk of state collapse in Pakistan and Afghanistan will increase, and violence will proliferate to Central Asia and South Asia, thus posing a major challenge to regional peace and stability. This chapter focuses on the assessment of prevailing security environment in the region, its implications for regional stability and measures needed for building a cooperative framework for sustainable peace and development in the region.

Assessment of Terrorism in the Region

Arc of Instability

A critical examination of the Human Development Indices (HDI) as shown in the table reveals that a number of countries in this region are highly impoverished and lie in the arc of instability.

Figure 2.1: Human Development Indices

Economic Indicators	*HDI*[1]	*Corruption*[2]	*GDP*[3]	*GDP (PPP)*[4]	*Fragile State*[5]
No. of Countries	(187)	(175)	(192)	(190)	(172)
Afghanistan	169	172	108	98	08
Pakistan	146	126	43	24	13
Iran	75	144	32	18	44
Uzbekistan	116	166	73	64	51
Kyrgyzstan	125	136	147	136	62
Tajikistan	133	152	140	134	57
Turkmenistan	103	169	86	83	78

Source: UNDP Report, released in 2014-15.

The poor HDI in these countries lend itself to the growth of radical ideologies and violence, thus compounding threat to humanitarian security.

Af-Pak Epicenter of International Terrorism

Taliban, al-Qaeda and their affiliates continue to pose a formidable threat to the region's security. These forces are adherents of a militant 'Salfi-Wahabi' ideology that seeks creation of a Caliphate, i.e. establishing Nizam-e-Mustafa (Sharia law). They are opposed to the concept of Westphalian democratic states and reject the concept of sovereignty of the people. They seek to expand their influence in the entire region by creating the mythical state of Khurasan, encompassing the territory of Caucasus, Central Asia, Xinjiang Province, Af-Pak region, Indian sub-continent etc. Outwardly, there are a number of Islamist radical groups that appear disparate and divergent in their objectives. Haqqani network, Hiz-e-Islami and Islamic State of Iraq and Syria (ISIS) are active in Afghanistan. Tehrik-e-Taliban of Pakistan (TTP), Jundullah and Jamaat-ul-Ahrar are fighting the Pakistan Government, whereas groups like Lashkar-e-Taiba, Hizul Mujahideen, Jaish-e-Mohamed, Jamat-ud-Dawa and al-Qaeda Indian sub-continent (AQIS) are protégé of ISI, directed against India. Sunni militant groups namely Sipah-e-Sahaba and Lashkar-e-Janghvi indulge in killing of Shia Muslims and other minorities. Likewise, groups like Islamic Movement of Uzbekistan (IMU), Uzbek Islamic Jihad, Hizb-e-Tehrir and Jund al-Khalifa are active in Central Asia and have linkages with Jaish al-Muhajireen wal Ansar active in Caucasus and East Turkistan Islamic Movement (ETIM), operating in the Xinjiang province. The experts believe that an array of terrorist outfits may pursue different tactical objectives but they are united in their overall ideological goal of creating a Caliphate. Therefore, their Pan-Islamist outlook propels them to forge alliances in favour of their larger religious cause. The assessment of terrorist network in Af-Pak region and Central Asia is briefly discussed in the succeeding paragraphs.

Situation in Pakistan

Pakistan has become a factory of terrorism. It is a garrison state with serious identity problem, and its military establishment exaggerates an existential threat from India. It harbours the notion of using the territory of Afghanistan for achieving strategic depth and sees Indian presence in Afghanistan as a design aimed at encirclement of Pakistan. It also strives to establish a pro–Pakistan regime in Afghanistan that accepts the Durand line as the border, thus mitigating its concerns of possible creation of state of Pakhtunistan, based on Pashtun nationalism that spans across Durand line. In pursuance of its strategic objectives, it uses terrorist network as an instrument of foreign policy to conduct asymmetric warfare against India and Afghanistan.

Despite President Ghani's outreach to Pakistan military establishment, setting aside protocol norms, Pakistan sponsored terrorism in Afghanistan has escalated. President Ghani and Afghan leaders are at pains to sensitise international community, how terrorists are attacking their country from their safe havens in Pakistan. In fact, Pakistan's much-touted ant-terrorist campaign (Zarb-e-Azb) has added to woes of Afghanistan. The Pakistan military establishment in their traditional duplicitous manner had issued warnings and given ample time to terrorists to vacate the areas astride Durand line and relocate themselves in Afghanistan. Spurt in terrorist strikes, particularly in the northern Afghanistan, is a direct outcome of Pakistan's flawed strategy. Similarly, Prime Minister Modi's overtures to break the deadlock in Indo-Pakistan dialogue through politico–diplomatic initiatives at Ufa, Bangkok and unprecedented calling on Nawaz Sharif at Lahore on his return from Kabul, were responded by sensational terrorist strikes against Indian consulates in Afghanistan and a series of terrorist strikes in India; attack on Pathankot airbase being the latest in the series of such attacks.

On the issue of fighting terrorism and improving relations with India and Afghanistan, there is a widening drift between the civil government and the all-powerful military establishment. There are broadly four categories of terrorists in Pakistan. First is the anti-state, namely TPP. This group has waged a war against the state and is responsible for spate of terrorists' strikes in Peshawar and Punjab, to name a few. TPP has also undertaken sensational strikes against education institutions and high profile military targets such as naval bases, air bases, military HQ and training establishment. Anti–state terrorist groups are competing with each other to strike Pakistan military branded by them as a 'Kafir' or infidel army; the splinter groups of this outfit owe allegiance to the ISIS. Pakistan has shown limited zeal to rein in masterminds of radicalism who are moving freely in the country. Series of attacks on churches on the eve of Easter in Lahore, in Shia Mosques and recent demonstrations in the wake of hanging of Mumtaz Qadri who had killed Punjab Provincial Governor Salman Taseer point towards growing radicalisation in the country. There is reluctance to crack down on the Punjab-based terror groups that enjoy political patronage. There is a fear that anti-terrorist operations in Punjab will have a serious political backlash for the government and military; its lower ranks do have radicalised elements. Ethno–regional faultlines and sectarian violence in Sindh, Baluchistan, Kyhber, Pakhtunkhwa, Punjab, Kashmir, Gilgit and Baltistan further exert a centrifugal pull to sweep Pakistan from nationalism to regionalism. The moot point is that Pakistan neither needs the American weapons nor the Chinese veto at the UN to bail it out from declaring some of its protégé as terrorists. It simply needs the international intervention to moderate its behaviour to put its house in order and stop unleashing terrorism against Afghanistan and India, and rest of the civilised world.

Situation in Afghanistan

Afghanistan is at critical crossroads of its strategic destiny. The fledgling state faces a myriad of challenges due to threat from Taliban while the country is mired in economic impoverishment, governance deficit and politico-ethnic drift. These challenges are compounded by the reduction of US and NATO forces. According to Nicholas Haysom, UN envoy to Afghanistan, survival will be an achievement for the National Unity Government (NUG) in 2016.[6]

He listed five challenges to the government: a contracting economy, low growth, high unemployment (25%), an intensifying insurgency and an increasing fractious and divided political environment. On the positive side, however, Afghanistan's geographic centrality makes it a strategic hub itself for transportation of trade and energy resources between Central Asia, West Asia and South Asia. A stable Afghanistan could thus change the geopolitical landscape of the entire region for the better. Afghanistan can also emerge as a rallying point for international fight against terrorism. In this regard, let me elaborate some key points:

- Afghanistan is facing serious economic and political challenges. Its foreign aid (97%)[7] and poppy-driven (50% of agriculture) economy needs a major revamping. Growth rate in Afghanistan has fallen from 14.4% in 2012 to 1.3% in 2014.[8] About 49% of the population lives below poverty line.[9] The Afghan government will have to modernise agriculture and encourage people to grow crops and develop agro-based industry. Education, health, infrastructure, employment, combating corruption and providing good governance will have to be the major thrust areas to lift millions of people from the morass of poverty to dignified living standards. Afghanistan is endowed with rich natural resources. A 2007 United States Geological Service survey appears to have discovered nearly USD 1 trillion in mineral deposits in Afghanistan.[10] The Afghan government, however, feels the value is around USD 3 trillion.[11] As per the survey, Afghanistan may hold 60 million tons of copper, 2.2 billion tons of iron ore, 1.4 million tons of rare earth elements such as lanthanum, cerium and neodymium, and lodes of aluminum, gold, silver, zinc, mercury and lithium. The mineral resources are yet to be fully surveyed and harnessed. Further, Afghanistan lacks rail and roadways infrastructure to transport its mineral resources. Hydropower is the main source of energy in Afghanistan. Due to prolonged war, power grids in Afghanistan are badly damaged. Only a third of the population has access to electricity. Afghanistan generates around 600 megawatts (MW) of electricity at present but as per Da Afghanistan Breshna Sherkat (DABS) estimates, the country will need around 3,000 MW to meet its needs by 2020.[12]

Afghanistan is reported to have oil reserves totaling 2.9 billion barrels and also produces natural gas.[13]

- Post-controversial Presidential elections, the politico-ethnic reconciliation between the President and CEO supporters has not taken place. Accord of constitutional legitimacy to appointment of CEO, conduct of parliamentary elections, Lohya Jirga and election reforms are pending. There is resentment in people against nepotism in making higher appointments in the government. The NUG has faced a wave of resignation in the recent weeks.

The portfolios of ministers of defence and interior and chief of the intelligence agency are lying vacant. There is a strong pro-Karzai group lobbying for the resignation of the President. The Council for Protection and Stability in Afghanistan, led by Abdul Rab Rasul Sayyaf and supported by estranged Mujahideen leaders, has targeted the government of President Ghani over corruption and election reforms.

According to the report of Special Inspector General for Afghanistan reconstruction, released on October 14, 2014, there has been a 50 percent increase in poppy-related proceeds from 2012 to 2013 despite the US spending $7 billion for poppy eradication.[14] Even provinces that were once declared poppy-free have seen resurgence in cultivation. Ironically, the production has increased due to the use of deep well technology in previously non–arable lands. Drug trafficking has been the main source of income for Taliban, warlords and corrupt-government officials. Drug addiction in Afghan society runs into generations since opium is taken as a medicine for relief of pain due to lack of medical facilities. Drug addiction, therefore, has had a phenomenal humanitarian security cost not only for Afghan society, but international community at large as well. Central Asia has emerged as a major drug trafficking conduit to Russia and Europe.

Narco-terrorism is a serious transnational threat that merits attention. Taliban are emboldened due to dedicated support from

Pakistan and lack of resolve of the international community to support the NUG. They have undertaken sensational strikes against High Value Strategic Targets. Out of nearly 400 Afghan districts, 38 districts are reportedly under Taliban control and 43 are being contested.[15] Taliban strongholds lie in Helmand in South, Logar and Wardak in East and Kunduz in North. As per James Clapper, director of US National Intelligence Agency, there would be escalation of violence by Taliban in 2016. Launch of spring offensive code-named Omari by Taliban bears testimony to this assessment. Dealing with factitious Taliban is a major challenge. As per Afghan security experts, there are about seven Taliban factions and many affiliates. Pakistan supported Mullah Akhtar Mohammad Mansur is dead, succeeded by deputies Mullah Haibatullah Akhundzada. Akhundzada and Sarajuddin Haqqani have intensified operations, and are not inclined for reconciliation talks. The second group, led by Mullah Mohammad Rasoul and his deputies (Mullah Manan Niazi and Mullah Baz Mohammad Haris), are more amenable to peace process albeit outside Pakistan prompting. There are a number of key Taliban leaders in Qatar, including Abbas Stanikazi (the head of the office), Mullah Jan Mohmmad Madani, Mullah Shahabudin Dilawar, Suhil Shanin, Mohmmad Zahid Ahmadzai, and Abdul Salam Hanafi. This office takes orders from Quetta Shura and is not encouraged by the NUG to deny them any political legitimacy. In sum, reconciliation talks with Taliban seem to be a non-starter. Taliban pre–conditions, such as withdrawal of foreign troops, lifting of ban that declared them as terrorists and non-participation in election process, are not acceptable. Sartaj Aziz, the foreign minister of Pakistan, during his recent visit to the US confessed that his country in not in total control of Taliban, implying thereby that it has limitations in nudging Taliban towards a reconciliation process. Besides these groups, there are about 5000 foreign rebels, including Arab, Chechen, Uzbek and Uighur fighters. These and some splinter groups of TTP have joined ranks of ISIS, which is active in Nagarhar province.

Creditably, Afghan National Security Forces (ANSF), despite serious capacity deficits, has put up stiff resistance to Taliban. There has been 50 percent increase in casualty rate to ANSF (14 per day). According to new US commanding general to Afghanistan, John Nicholson, during 2015, 5,500 Afghan troops were killed and more than 14,000 were wounded.[16] There are about 3600 deserters in the ANSF. Intelligence, surveillance and reconnaissance, aerial and artillery support, leadership crisis, logistics stamina, training etc. are the major grey areas in ANSF. In Afghanistan, US/NATO will maintain 9,800 troops till 2016 and about 5,500 troops till 2017, in addition to 12000 NATO troops till 2020. General Nicholson has declared strategic shift operations supported by airpower and mobilising logistics surge capability for the beleaguered Afghan units. There is growing realisation that the further withdrawal of troops should not be based on imaginary timelines but on actual operational conditions existing on ground. International economic and military aid is the key to the survival of NUG and maintaining organisational cohesiveness of ANSF. The total budget of NUG is approximately $10 billion, whereas its revenue is approximately $4 billion. They need $5/6 billion uninterrupted foreign aid. In contrast, Taliban need about $400 million annually, wrenched from drug money and extortions to keep their arms supply and payment to their cadres.[17] Incidentally, Taliban pay much higher amount to their cadres than what is paid to the Afghan officers and soldiers.[18] As per experts, if no foreign aid arrives, the NUG may at best be able to survive for about three years before its collapse the Najib regime way, which lasted barely three years after foreign aid stopped between 1993-1996. Afghanistan may not face a 1996-type of crisis this time over due to lack of public support to Taliban and resistance from a better trained ANSF. Also, the factitious Taliban will lack over support from Pakistan due to international pressure. But, in the absence of international support, Afghanistan will plunge deeper into chaos, thus lending itself to ethnic strife and tug of war between warlords.

Situation in Central Asia

Geospatially and historically, Af-Pak region and Central Asia are part of the same strategic space. Afghanistan shares porous borders with Tajikistan (1344 km), Uzbekistan border (137 km) and Turkmenistan (744 km). Demographically, there are close ethnic linkages between Central Asians and Afghanistan. Out of 31 million-population of Afghanistan, Pashtun are 42%, Tajiks 27%, Hazaras 9%, Uzbek 9% and Turkmens 3%.[19] Afghanistan assumes significant importance in the security calculus of Russia, China and Central Asian States. Afghanistan was at the center-stage of Great Game of the 19th century between Great Britain and Russia, which culminated into its status as a strategic buffer between the two major powers. In the 20th century, Afghanistan again witnessed a virulent conflict between the Soviet Union and the US that saw legitimisation of Islamic terrorism and eventually turning Af-Pak region as an epicenter of international terrorism. In the wake of the break-up of Soviet Union, during the civil war in Tajikistan, many Islamist fighters were operating from Afghanistan. Subsequently, IMU had launched from its safe havens in Afghanistan operations in 1999-

2001 to topple regime in Uzbekistan; and in 2003, carried out terrorist strikes in Tashkent. Fergana valley is a flash point for intra and inter-state conflicts over unresolved border disputes between Uzbekistan and its neighbours; contentions over sharing of water between upper and lower riparian states besides ethnic strife are common. Civil war in Tajikistan in 1992, Tulip Revolutions in Kyrgyzstan, Andijan Uprising in 2005 in Uzbekistan and ethnic clashes in 2010 in Kyrgyzstan are stark reminders of the fragile security scenario in the region. The region also faces problems of narco-terrorism and risk of nuclear-terrorism due to access to orphan fissile material that could be used for making low-yield radiation bombs. Political transition and succession of aging political rulers is a major tipping point that can trigger socio-political crises.

Implications for Regional Stability

It needs no emphasis that failure of ANSF and Pakistan to contain resurgent Taliban and other terrorist outfits will have serious consequences for the Af-Pak region, with wider ramifications for the Indian sub-continent, Central Asia, Xinjiang province and Caucasus. Escalation of violence and radicalisation are fraught with risks of state collapse in Pakistan and Afghanistan. Particularly susceptible to terrorist influence is Fergana valley in Central Asia, where the traditionally orthodox population faces a perceived sense of relative deprivation and ethnic divide. Complicated succession of unstable regimes in Central Asia can inadvertently provide a spark to ignite the situation, thus setting the stage for terrorists to fish in troubled waters. De-stabilisation of Af–Pak region, Central Asia and Xinjiang province will have unintended consequences for China's One Road-One Belt project, flow of energy resources from the Caspian region and operationalisation of China-Pakistan Economic Corridor (CPEC). Likewise, emboldened terrorists have potential to escalate violence in Kashmir, push India-Pakistan towards a military confrontation, heighten the risk of nuclear terrorism and scuttle the prospects of Turkmenistan-Afghanistan-Pakistan–India (TAPI) and Iran–Pakistan–India (IPI) pipelines as well as Central Asia South Asia Electricity Transmission and Trade project (CASA 1000 MW) electricity project. Therefore, it is crucial that the regional countries are cognizant of this larger trans-national threat that can destabilise the region. Hence, the defeat of Taliban in Af-Pak region is a sine qua non for regional security.

More pertinent in this regard is the role of Pakistan, which has thus far used these terrorists as instrument of state policy to pursue its perceived strategic interests against India and Afghanistan. It is high time Pakistan realises that chickens have come home to roost. Today, the Government of Pakistan considers terrorist violence as principal threat to its national security. After Zarb-e-Azb it is now contemplating launching counter- terrorism operations in Punjab. However, its policy of supporting Haqqani network in Afghanistan and anti-India terrorist groups has not changed. It's about time

Pakistan changed its mindset and shedits duplicity in dealing with different militant outfits differently. I must caution here that in the past, the US and the West-ignored Af-Pak region faced the consequences of terrorism in the US and Europe. Inept handling of crises in West Asia has not only plunged the region in serious crisis but also made it a strong bastion of radical ideology and despotic ISIS as a potent trans–national threat that has spread its tentacles to Europe. Sagacity demands that the regional countries and the United States-led West shed their selective approaches in dealing with terrorism and work towards a collaborative framework to curb this serious menace to humanitarian security.

Towards Collaboration in Combating Terrorism

India is a major stakeholder in peace and development in the Af-Pak region. India, for decades, has been a victim of state-sponsored terrorism. India considers early fructification of energy and trade corridors from Central Asia via Afghanistan and Iran to South Asia, which is vital for its comprehensive national development. The country has made significant contribution towards peace building in Afghanistan by assisting the ANSF in capacity-building and constructing civil infrastructure. India has spent about $2 billion on various projects in Afghanistan, and is committed to support the new Afghan government under the aegis of strategic partnership agreement signed between the two countries in November 2011. India is against any Zero- Sum outlook on Afghanistan and favours an inclusive and collaborative approach to peace building in the country. She is also ready to undertake joint development projects with Pakistan and other countries.

Looking from a broader strategic perspective, building cooperation to fight terrorism in the Af-Pak region and its neighbourhood is plausibly a win-win paradigm. The selective approach of US-led West operations in Afghanistan has achieved limited results that appear unsustainable. Likewise, the Quadrilateral Coordination Group (QCG) comprising Pakistan, China, the US and Afghanistan has not succeeded in reconciliation with intransigent Taliban. In the meanwhile, the Shanghai Cooperation Organisation (SCO), with the entry of India and Pakistan, and Afghanistan and Iran being active observers, has emerged as the most formidable regional grouping dealing with the regional security and development issues. The SCO should earnestly work on sharing of intelligence, combating narco-terrorism, nuclear-terrorism, curbing terror-financing networks, cyber security, capacity building, interoperability and conducting counter–terrorism exercises. Key to fighting terrorism lies in undertaking joint counter-terrorism operations by Afghanistan and Pakistan along the Durand line, and dismantling the terrorist infrastructure there as well. In these endeavours, India can bring to bear its live operational experience in counter-insurgency and counter-terrorism operations to the SCO forum. Likewise, Russia and three Central Asian states (Kazakhstan, Tajikistan and Kyrgyzstan) are members of the Collective Security Organisations (CSTO). Both these organisation have established Anti-Terrorists Centres in Central Asia and regularly conduct joint military training to combat terrorism. On the other hand, NATO, under the Programme for Peace (PfP), is engaged in capacity-building against non-traditional threats in the region. The regional leadership and these organisations should assiduously shed their traditional mindsets and explore avenues for creating a collaborative security framework and mechanisms to foster cooperation between NATO, SCO and CSTO to fight terrorism.

Conclusion

Peace building in Afghanistan should be Afghan-owned and Afghan-led. The NUG will have to create an investor-friendly climate to attract foreign investors in mining and other resource sectors. Afghanistan needs sustained external aid, technical expertise and dedicated commitment from the international community, along with efficient management of funds at home by the political and administrative establishment. The international community and major donors of Afghanistan should tie their aid and economic assistance programs to key reforms in the public institutions such as fighting corruption, reforming of the judiciary, implementing the rule of law, improving subnational governance and improving Afghanistan's public financial management system.

END NOTES

1. Based on UNDP Report, released in 2014, 2013 rankings http://hdr.undp.org/en/content/table-1-human-development-index-and-its-components
2. Corruption Perceptions Index 2013, released by Transparency International in 2014, http://www.transparency.org/cpi2013/results
3. World Bank GDP ranking (2013 figures) released in 2014 http://databank.worldbank.org/data/download/GDP.pdf
4. World Bank GDP PPP ranking (2013 figures) released in 2014 http://databank.worldbank.org/data/download/GDP_PPP.pdf
5. Fragile State Index 2014 Index http://ffp.statesindex.org/rankings-2014
6. 'Survival will be an achievement' for new Afghan Government, says UN envoy, March 15, 2016, available at http://www.un.org/apps/news/story.asp?NewsID=53448#.VzK6B9R97Gg.
7. Economic depression' looms in Afghanistan, *Al Jazeera*, 8 June, 2011, available at http://www.aljazeera.com/news/asia/2011/06/20116812933228775.html
8. World Bank Data, available at http://data.worldbank.org/indicator/NY.GDP.MKTP.KD.ZG/countries/AF?display=graph
9. Ghani says al-Qaeda, Taliban and ISIS threaten Afghanistan, *Khaama Press*, April 4, 2016, available at http://www.khaama.com/ghani-terror-groups-including-al-qaeda-taliban-and-isis-threaten-afghanistan-0535
10. Rare Earth: Afghanistan Sits on $1 Trillion in Minerals, *NBC News*, September 5, 2014, available at http://www.nbcnews.com/science/science-news/rare-earth-afghanistan-sits-1-trillion-minerals-n196861
11. Afghanistan claims mineral wealth is worth $3 trillion, *The Telegraph*, 17 June, 2010, available at http://www.telegraph.co.uk/news/worldnews/asia/afghanistan/7835657/Afghanistan-claims-mineral-wealth-is-worth-3trillion.html
12. Electricity only reaches one in three Afghans, *Reuters*, January 9, 2012, available at http://www.reuters.com/article/us-afghanistan-power-idUSTRE8080C920120109
13. https://en.wikipedia.org/wiki/Energy_in_Afghanistan#Natural_gas_and_oil
14. $7 Billion US Eradication Effort Delivers Record High Poppy Crop in Afghanistan, October 21, 2014, available at http://www.common

dreams.org/news/2014/10/21/7-billion-us-eradication-effort-delivers-record-high-poppy-crop-afghanistan

15. Available at https://www.google.com/maps/d/u/0/viewer?mid=10Qz0dzwDWpj6bkfyWN6qoLIhaaU
16. Exclusive: Fierce Afghan fighting slows NATO training mission - new U.S. commander, *Reuters*, April 4, 2016, available at http://www.reuters.com/article/us-afghanistan-security-exclusive-idUSKCN0X11MO
17. How the Taliban get their money, January 21, 2016, available at http://www.dw.com/en/how- the-taliban-get-their-money/a-18995315
18. Taliban Fighters Paid 4,000 AFS Per Day, 16 September 2014, available at http://english.cheraghdaily.org/index.php/taliban-fighters-paid-4-000-afs-per-day
19. https://en.wikipedia.org/wiki/Afghanistan

Chapter 3

External Powers in Central Asia

Ibrahim Koncak

Introduction

Central Asia (CA), with its grand landmass, natural resources, ancient history as a bridge between the West and East, and once, as the center of land powers before the discovery of sea-lanes, is in the process of establishing its place and identity in enhanced areas such as economy, politics, geopolitics, culture and technology. CA is not only in the process of establishing its identity on an international level, but also on national level with peculiarities in each state within the region. There are two waves or levels of foundational processes going on in the region, with probabilistic effects reaching far beyond the region.

First, internationally, major powers such as Russia, China, India and the EU are having an ebb-and-flow approach in their policies towards the region. That's to say, too precious to leave aside-too early to hop in situation is leaving them in limbo. Excluding China's mega-infrastructural investments in terms of energy transfer and Russia's military presence, major powers do not seem to be eager to provide full-scale, long-term economic, military and technological investments and guarantees to the region. CA is not in the center of foreign policy objectives of these powers, for reasons stemming from lack of infrastructure of transfer routes and/or the anxiety of jeopardising their interest vis-à-vis each other on other regions and issues. Nonetheless, the geopolitical structuring process is underway with small but sure steps taken by the involved states.

Second, regional states within CA are in the foundational process of nation and identity-building in quiet specific ways and means. Although commonly Turkic, the nation/state-building process seems to be requiring them to focus on differences rather than similarities. Also, regimes of the countries are making the situation unique and exceptional; swaying from authoritarian to parliamentary democracy. These on-going international and regional processes are, to some extent, hindering regional integration and slowing down the progress in completing region's integration with the world. Despite differences, all regional states are seeking to connect with the outside world in multiple ways. Taking into consideration the growing population in Asia and seemingly economic and technological shift from the West to the East, CA seems to have the potential to play a vital role in economic and geopolitical terms in decades ahead.

This chapter focuses on the role of major powers in shaping the external and internal policies of the CA states, and also the response of the states within the region toward the policies of involved countries. It highlights how above-mentioned double-edged processes affect the outcome of policy initiatives. Policies of major powers such as Russia, China and the United States are evaluated in terms of high level official visits. The possible role of great-to-medium powers in internal and external policies of CA states is analysed with considerable focus on perspectives from CA. The ratio of high level official visits conducted by the representatives of involved states to the CA countries is taken as an indicator to demonstrate the interest toward the region vis-à-vis each other. In foreign policy discourses, "New Great Game" is densely debated by pundits and policy makers. How scholars and elites in CA perceive and respond to the rhetoric of the Great Games is explained in detail.

The Role of Geography on Foreign Policies

Central Asia, located in the heart of the Eurasian landmass, extending from the Caspian Sea in the West to the border of modern China in the East and occupying an area of 3,994.400 square kilometers, is landlocked area with appealing natural resources and newly independent sister states. Geographic location of the states, as all other factors without doubt, affect foreign policy formation of the states in the age of globalisation and interdependence, and the states of CA are no exception to this. States in CA define their foreign policy priorities in accordance with the geographic proximity; that is to say from adjacent neighbours to neighbouring super powers and to distant states with substantial interest in the region in terms of economy, security and energy[1]. The landlocked status of the states within CA is obliging them to maintain a balance (difficult at times though) between neighbouring major powers such as Russia and China, and in their foreign policies and economic relations as well. Furthermore, they are all dependent on each other within the region.

In the study of challenges stemming from being landlocked, Faye and his associates (2004) argue that landlocked countries have lower level of human development and external trade compared with nautical neighbours, as they depend on transit neighbours for trade, infrastructure, political relations, administrative practices and stability in the neighbouring countries[2]. Paradoxically, when it comes to CA, the situation is far more complicated than other landlocked regions due to the fact that states within the region lack efficient legal infrastructure despite shared economic history during the Soviet era. Nevertheless, the CA states are remarkably complementary to each other geographically, historically, politically and economically[3]. Shared water resources, intricately delimited, even in case of Uzbekistan, Kyrgyzstan and Tajikistan not demarcated, borders and enclaves with simmering disputes contribute regional foreign policy formation more than anywhere else. The geography not only affects the policies of the states toward each other within the region, but also with other states around the region.

As Starr (2011) puts it, CA is important when taking into consideration neighbours such as Afghanistan, China, Russia and Iran from American perspective. As such, the surrounding regions and states are indispensably vital for the states of CA for their political and economic security. The elites in CA are well aware that the economic development, more importantly stability and security in their states, is at stake; and so, they formulate their foreign policies accordingly. In terms of economy, as Kazakh foreign minister Erlan Idrissov puts it: "Central Asia is not landlocked but land linking", stressing the revival of ancient Silk Road with new means and policies[4]. From the very beginning, as the states in the region gained their independence, the elites of the states have been vigilant in taking into consideration the geographical locations of their countries to formulate their foreign policies. Namely, as elsewhere, geography plays a major role in the foreign policy formation of CA states toward each other, and toward other surrounding countries.

Great Games or Great Gains

In the rhetoric of scholars, the term 'New Great Game' has been much frequently pronounced following the collapse of the Soviet Union, and it is still the case[5]. The term is based on erroneous assumption due to lack of relevant information on newly independent states. The assumption was that there would be "power vacuum" in CA without any major power controlling the region, and the outcome would be a new great game as the one in the 19th century between Russian and British empires. Research following the demise of the Soviet Union revealed that there had been state and identity building, not sovereign in CA from 1924 onwards culminating in 1980s though[6]. The analogy made between the "Big Game" of 19th century and the so called "New Big Game" in this century has problems in itself.

First of all, the so-called Big Game between Russian and British empires were not exactly for CA itself, but perceived threat assessment and suspicions of these powers toward each other. Khanates of CA from the perspective of relations toward major powers seem to be passive, and antagonistic toward each other. The Khanates were much protective against outsiders and suspicious of any attempt from Russians and the British, thus always keeping the doors locked for any cooperation other than limited trade in the age of invasions. Secondly, with the collapse of the Soviet Union, we did not have Khanates anymore on the stage, but well-established nation states with dedicated elite and cultivated people to carry on the formation of nation / state-building further. Moreover, the governments of the new independent states have been extremely active and collaborative toward major and medium powers. The extensive number of official visits done by presidents and head of governments to other countries reflect that openness and political will to integrate with the world in multiple directions.

Another difficult point for the claim of the "New Big Game" is that it is the difficulty, and lack of empirical data; official government statements either within CA or involved states such as Russia, the US, China, India and others stress more cooperation rather than confrontation when it comes to CA. We have coinciding interests rather than clash of interests, as all sides want stable a CA, and threat of terrorism, extremism and drug trafficking is perceived as threat by states within CA and abroad. The new circumstances in the era of interdependence are paving the way for more cooperation and serving the interests of the states more than confrontation. From the perspective of Central Asian countries, Great Gains which represent them as subjects is much more attractive than Great Games denoting them as objects.

The governments of the Central Asian counties have been careful not to cause the emergence of any kind of confrontational environment within the region among major powers. It can be seen clearly from the large number of inter-governmental organisations membered and hosted by Central Asian states backed by either

Russia in case of Common Wealth of Independent States (CIS), Collective Security Treaty Organisation (CSTO), Eurasian Customs Union or China in case of Shanghai Cooperation Organisation (SCO), or Turkey with Turkic Council. In addition, the states are either partner or member in many other organisations on different levels and calibers. International structure along with the deliberate policies of the individual states is enforcing balance among the major powers in CA. And Central States are responding that with collaborative and consciously formed relations positively. From this perspective, once more, CA is becoming the center of diversity and debate with slowly laid infrastructural base.

Today, mega projects are underway either on the field or on paper in and through CA. Pipelines such as Turkmenistan–China gas pipeline, Kazakhstan-China oil pipeline. The Turkmenistan-Afghanistan-Pakistan-India gas pipeline (TAPI), newly-built or planned highways and railways are all laying the ground for the revival of Silk Roads with new dimensions and visions. As once, the epicenter of the first waves of globalisation, connecting eastern and western markets, cultural and religious traditions[7], CA is underway to become the unparalleled transit land in the age of new globalisation with much more penetrating effects than the first one. The transition from confined landlocked-ness to revealing land linking is not only economic, but also traditional and cultural.

Speech given at Rumi Forum, Fedric Starr (November 28, 2013)[8] argues:

> "The rich background of the Arab world is key to this talk; the variety of religions, Zoroastrianism and the presence of Alexander the Great. This amalgamation of cultures led CA to become the epicenter of religions, great intellect and unparalleled enterprise. Strong trade ties and a passion to create, rather than import, led to the region becoming a vast silk exporter and the creator of cotton paper. This vibrant intellectual and cultural world was a victim of religious controversy. The long period of prosperity and scientific thought was brought to an end by the presence of an increasingly orthodox population. This suspicion hindered the pursuit of scientific research, as it was increasingly

> believed that the Quran exclusively held the answers to all of life's questions".[9]

Nowadays, throughout CA—in mosques, churches, institutes, universities and many other venues initiated and supported by either Central Asians or others from different parts of the world—one can observe extraordinary bustle going on. What may be the outcome of such an immense activity, positive or negative, is difficult to predict at this stage. But one can assume that CA is becoming the café of ideas and ideologies as the caravan *sarays* of the vivid ancient Silk Road era. That CA is or will be the arena of Great Games or splendid bazaars of Great Gains depends on the policy course taken by states within CA and surrounding countries. From Central Asians' perspective, it's not a game but struggle for survival in the economic, security and political sense. We can see that in statements of the officials of Central Asian states.

In his article titled 'Great Gain, not Great Game in Central Asia', Erlan Idrissov, foreign minister of Kazakhstan (2016), states: "It has, for example, become increasingly popular for journalists to see events in our region through the prism of a revival of the Great Game in CA. It is through this narrative of major powers fighting for influence that recent visits by the leaders of China, Russia, India, Pakistan, Japan, as well as the United States are seen".

These countries and their leaders all want to strengthen their relationships with Kazakhstan—as we do with them—as a partner and friend. As US Secretary John Kerry explained, for example, that the US is not pursuing a "zero-sum game" in central Eurasia but believes that greater engagement by all will benefit everyone. This is a message which we wholeheartedly welcome, and which I hope all those watching and commenting on Kazakhstan will hear.

At this stage, one can confidently claim that as long as states within CA respond to the major powers' policies toward CA with cooperative balancing policies, as has been so far with some slight deviation in the case of Bakiyev period in Kyrgyzstan[10] and can sustain their balancing policies successfully in the decades ahead,

CA will revive economically, culturally and scientifically. As already stated above the mega projects, internationally-sponsored universities, institutes, inter-governmental and non-governmental organisations, Muslim, Christian and other missionaries are forming a diverse environment with potential coexistence and conflict.

Meanwhile, how major powers assess and formulate their policies toward the region in general, and each individual regional state in particular, may shift the existing internal and external balance to some hazardous setting in which ethnic and interstate wars may occur. That's to say; up until now, as close neighbour China has played down its role with very active contract policy, and with Russia using more assertive rhetoric. Nonetheless, in the foreseeable future, that kind of confrontation or proxy war in CA seems unlikely. Since from economic and political perspective, China and Russia need each other more than they both need CA, the two powers would hardly enter confrontational rivalry to any extent to jeopardise their relations and interests in other areas. The United States and European Union (EU) as distant powers mostly depend on allies and partners in their policies and interests in CA.

Two factors are hindering the full scale direct involvement of the US and European Union (EU) in economic and security affairs: 1) Due to high risks of investment, especially for large scale initiatives and lack of integration within the region, big companies have not shown any interest to invest in CA; 2) The US is much more focused on Southeast Asia, and the EU has got its eyes on Ukraine. They would hardly wish to get in any sort of confrontation on CA with China and Russia. Moreover, economically, when Central Asian and Southeast Asian trade and economic capacity are compared, it would not be rational to get into altercation and cause alliance formation between Russia and China. Furthermore, taking into consideration the low price of oil in world markets, major power confrontation on CA in decade(s) ahead is unlikely. But that does not mean that the region has not been so important in the eyes of major powers, since the number of official visits from and to CA underlines the region's importance.

Shuttle Diplomacy

Following independence, presidents of five Central Asian countries undertook intense shuttle diplomacy toward many countries and succeeded in becoming the focus of international community. The visits yielded wide range of political and economic gains, and positive response from major and medium powers. Since the independence of five republics of CA, high level visits from Russia, China, Turkey, Iran and other states has been laying ground for integration process of CA with the globe. Although criticised by some commentators for being only on paper, signed agreements opened the interaction and dialogue channels between the regional states and outside powers.

High level visits and signed agreements are important to show the level of relations between states. There is regularity and continuity of visits to the region from Russia and China. Comparing the number of visits at presidential level, the United States is far behind Russia and China, which indicates the place of CA in these countries' foreign policy objectives. The official visits are opening high level communication channels and further deepening the relations and forming diversifying environment as well as balancing the geopolitical formation in the region. As some scholars argue, the visits are serving the legitimacy of the governments as outside support to some regimes in the region from democratic perspective[11]. Classifying Central Asian states according to foreign policy directions, one can observe three trends: pro-Russian in case of Kyrgyzstan and Tajikistan, especially last five to six years; pro-Chinese in case of Uzbekistan, and neutrality and balance in case of Turkmenistan and Kazakhstan. Although this classification does not convey the exact trends of these countries' foreign policy directions, it provides rational and logical meaning to the analytical base of the study matter.

Presidential level visits from China to five Central Asian countries are not less than those of Russia. Chinese visits are more economy-oriented in terms of energy agreements compared with Russian visits, which include diverse topics from economy to security. The US visits are mainly security-oriented with less economic ingredient.

From major power standpoint, CA is not an arena of harsh rivalry, even though mild jealousy exists. But from regional perspective, CA may be hot-bed of conflicts and disputes unless some sort of sustainable regional integration is established between the five Central Asian states. The visits of Russia and China far exceed the USA and other powers in terms of the scope of the visits and signed agreements and protocols to cement the interstates relations. The role of great powers in shaping the regional is as real as the relations between the states within the region.

Often, the five Central Asian leaders meet with the leaders of Russia and China, but almost never among themselves. As mentioned earlier, the geography is forcing the states to work together, at least high level diplomatic channels be opened with regular summits among the leaders to discuss border, water usage and ethnic issues. Namely, some sort of functioning, even with limited regional integration, has the potential to keep the geopolitical and geo-economics balance internationally and regionally.

Conclusion

CA is the heart of the Eurasian landmass with consequential potential to become a bridge as officials and pundits from CA wish; or the hotbed of conflicts and the source of geopolitical rivalry accompanied by instability and/or proxy war zone if not dealt with delicacy by major powers and regional states as well. Thus far, the balance has been kept due to marginality of the region in foreign policies of the neighbouring major powers and the United States of America (USA), in addition to integrative policy approaches of states in CA, which has served to their interests and secured their independence with considerable economic and political benefits. The geography is playing one of the major roles in foreign policy of the states within CA and policy of major powers towards CA. In terms of official visits and concluded agreements with realisable potential, Russia and China are far ahead than any other state, including the USA. Central Asian elites stress bridge role than the role of geopolitical cliff and full scale integration with the outside world, though not so enthusiastic, with the exception of Kyrgyzstan and Tajikistan, to integration within CA. Nevertheless, some sort of functions, even though limited integration within CA, is needed more than anything else in the region.

END NOTES

1. Omelicheva Y.M., "Counterterrorism Policies in Central Asia", Routledge, 2010, p. 99.
2. Ibid., pp. 44-49.
3. Kembayev Z., "Legal Aspects of Regional Integration in Central Asia", *Zaö RV* 66 , 2006, pp. 967-983.
4. Horton S. "How Central is Central Asia?", Part 3/3, *You Tube*, available at https://www.youtube.com/watch?v=9D_ZjHHi1vo, October 29, 2010.
5. Cooley A., "Great Games, Local Rules: The New Power Contest in Central Asia", Oxford University Press, 2012, pp. 3-7.
6. Omelicheva Y.M., "Counterterrorism Policies in Central Asia", Routledge, 2010, pp. 148-149.
7. McBridge J., "Building the New Silk Road, Council on Foreign Affairs", available at http://www.cfr.org/asia-and-pacific/building-new-silk-road/p36573
8. S. Frederick Starr, "Central Asia's Golden Age: What Was It and What is Its Meaning Today?," available at http://rumiforum.org/central-asias-golden-age-what-was-it-and-what-is-its-meaning- today-with-s-frederick-starr/
9. Ibid.
10. Cooley A., "Great Games, Local Rules: The New Power Contest in Central Asia", Oxford University Press, 2012, pp. 120-122.
11. "Delegation of the Commission of the European Communities", *Europe*, Issue 403, 2001, p. 28.

Chapter 4

Role of Great Powers in Central Asia

Nivedita Das Kundu

Introduction

The Central Asian region emerged after the collapse of the Soviet Union and formed five independent states: Kazakhstan, Uzbekistan, Turkmenistan, Kyrgyzstan and Tajikistan. Origins of these states also date back to the USSR, when in 1920s-1930s, they were established as separate Soviet Republics and their borders were drawn by Soviet Commissars of Nationalities according to the ethnic lines. The countries of the region have a common history and culture, which contributes to the perception of Central Asia as a single region. With regard to the political and economic processes, kinship among these five countries is quite low to call the area a single region. After the independence, all these countries faced serious political and economic challenges. Despite the similarity of problems, each state sought solutions in different ways and showcased different development outcomes. In spite of the fact that it has now been more than 20 years since they got their independence, the countries of the region have been unable to establish significant regional alliances. Any form of associations involving all regional states has been possible only with the participation of third actors that are the external powers. Russia and China have played a catalytic role in bringing these countries together in SCO, with the aim to ensure security and stability in the region. Russia and China are the major players in the region, both have wide-ranging interests and enjoy significant levers of influence in the region. The United States of America also has greater interest and had significant influence, even though it has reduced to certain extent by now. Involvement of regional big players such as Turkey, Iran and India are also significant, and looking for ways for more active cooperation with these states.[1] The following paragraphs of this chapter provide overview of the role of great powers in Central Asia, focusing on general discourse on the topic.

Russia-Central Asia

Originally, when the region gained independence after the demise of the former Soviet Union, it was clear that Russia would consider this region as a natural extension of the area for its own national interests. In 1992, Russia announced the doctrine of the "near abroad", according to which the countries of the former Soviet Union have been declared as Russia's sphere of political and economic interest.

Central Asian states were no exception and Russia paid more attention to this region than to other post-Soviet states, and was even referred to as "underbelly of Russia". This region was considered a 'buffer zone', which secures Russia's southern borders[2], and Russia became a guarantor for maintaining stability and security of the region.

Presently, there are approximately seven million ethnic Russians living in Central Asian countries.[3] Russia uses the influence of Russian language and human ties, which consequently enables them to easily influence the public opinion in the region. Existence of Russian military forces in the Central Asia states is another lever, as well as sign of "special attitudinal relationship" with Russia. Russia has considerable military force in the region, including Kant airbase, anti-submarine weapons testing Centre in Issyk-Kul Lake and few laboratories and communication nods in Kyrgyzstan, military base in Tajikistan (the largest Russian base abroad with approximately 7000 soldiers), Sary Shagan anti-ballistic missile testing rage, Balkhash-9 Radar Station, Kastanay military-transportation airbase in Kazakhstan and some other military establishments in the Central Asian countries.[4]

Currently, more than 3.5 million labour migrants from Central Asia work in Russia, and Russia uses this as a tool for negotiations. Besides security concerns, Russia also has economic interests in the region, mostly focused in energy area. Until opening of Chinese pipelines in 2009-2010, almost all energy export corridors from the Central Asian states to the world markets used to pass through the territory of Russia.[5]

Moreover, Russia's main rail and highways are vital for facilitating Central Asia's trade with western markets, which makes Central Asian states vulnerable to Russia to a certain extent.[6] Russia involved Central Asian states in the multilateral regional structures that it has initiated, mainly the regional security and economic cooperation organisations like Shanghai Cooperation Organisation (SCO), Eurasian Economic Union (EEU), East Asia Economic Caucus (EAEC) and Collective Security Treaty Organisation (CSTO) etc.[7] Russia's geopolitical presence in this vast region remains strong, Russia is comparatively the most influential foreign actor in Central Asia, but it understands the limits of its ability. Hence, Russia can be relatively strong, but no more a full-fledged dominant external power in Central Asia.

China–Central Asia

Since independence of five Central Asian states, several Confucius institutes have been opened-up in the capitals of Central Asian states (aimed at teaching Mandarin language), which is China's "soft power" card. China views Central Asia as an important source for hydro-carbon imports that could reduce Beijing's risky dependency on maritime routes.[8] China doesn't consider it worthwhile to challenge Russia in Central Asia; rather, it prefers the strategy of

Fig. 5.1: Map of Russia's and United States' Military Installations in Kyrgyzstan

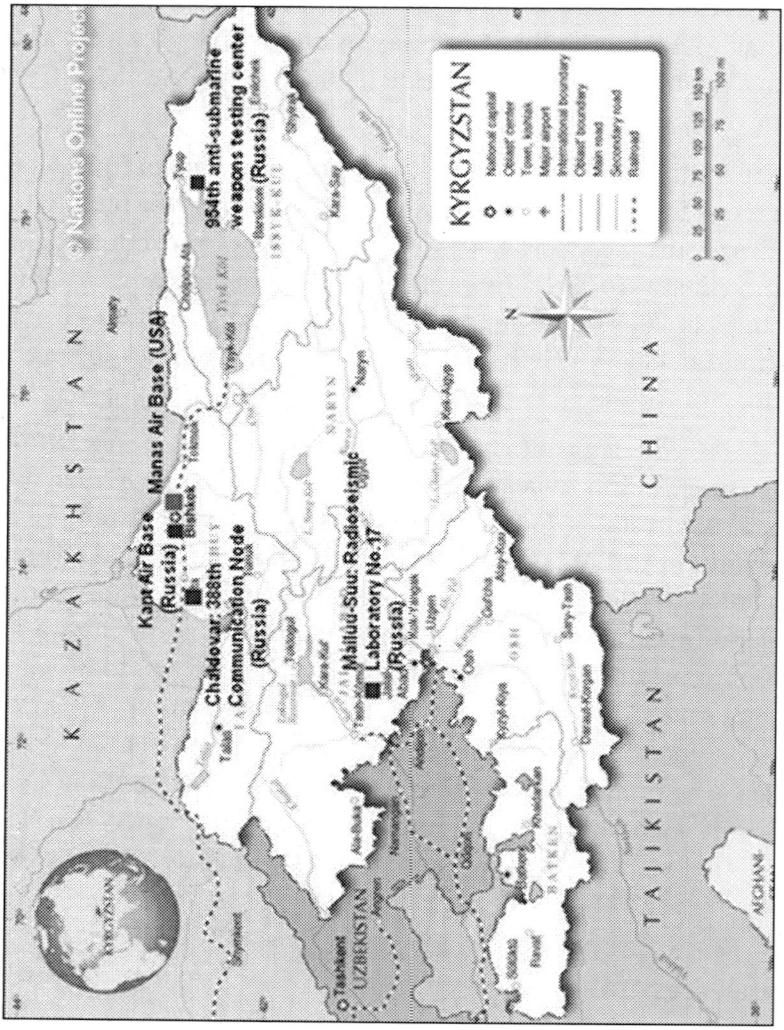

Source: http://www.nationsonline.org/oneworld/map/kyrgyzstan-administrative-map.htm

gradual increase in economic penetration and political cooperation with the region, balancing its relations with Russia. The Central Asian countries try to use China for diversifying their foreign relations, export markets and investment sources.[9] Central Asian states recognises the possible dangers of rising "Chinese expansionism" in the region, and certain China-phobia is already present among the population in the Central Asian countries and seeks ways for firmly ensuring their long-term sovereignty.

United States-Central Asia

It has been more than a decade after the 9/11 attacks for United States of America (USA), and the war in Afghanistan has been the point of reference for USA's policy toward the Central Asian States. US military bases in regions like Karatog (Tajikistan), Almaty (Kazakhstan) and Manas (Kyrgyzstan) (even though the situation has now changed after the lease period of Manas Airbase expired in 2014), shows its reasonable influence over the region. Central Asia's role in facilitating the supply chain for US and NATO troops to Afghanistan were the main focus of the US policy throughout the period.[10] Uzbekistan's Karshi-Khanabad Airbase and Kyrgyzstan's Manas Airbase have both hosted US military installations and troops supporting Afghan combat operations. Washington also helped Central Asian states to establish new energy transportation and supply routes that bypass Russia in order to reduce Russia's dominance in the region.[11] During mid-2000, certain events like "colour revolutions", US backing for regime change in Kyrgyzstan and promotion of civil society, Andijan event as well as Russia's gradual resurgence due to the immense energy revenues helped to change the atmosphere in Central Asia, and questioned US goals in the region and re-oriented Central Asian states foreign policy toward Russia.[12]

Washington intensified contacts with the Central Asian countries located on the Northern Distribution Network (NDN) routes. However, Central Asia became less central to US foreign and security policy following the drawdown of forces in Afghanistan.

Fig. 5.2: Map of Major United States Logistic Routes to Afghanistan

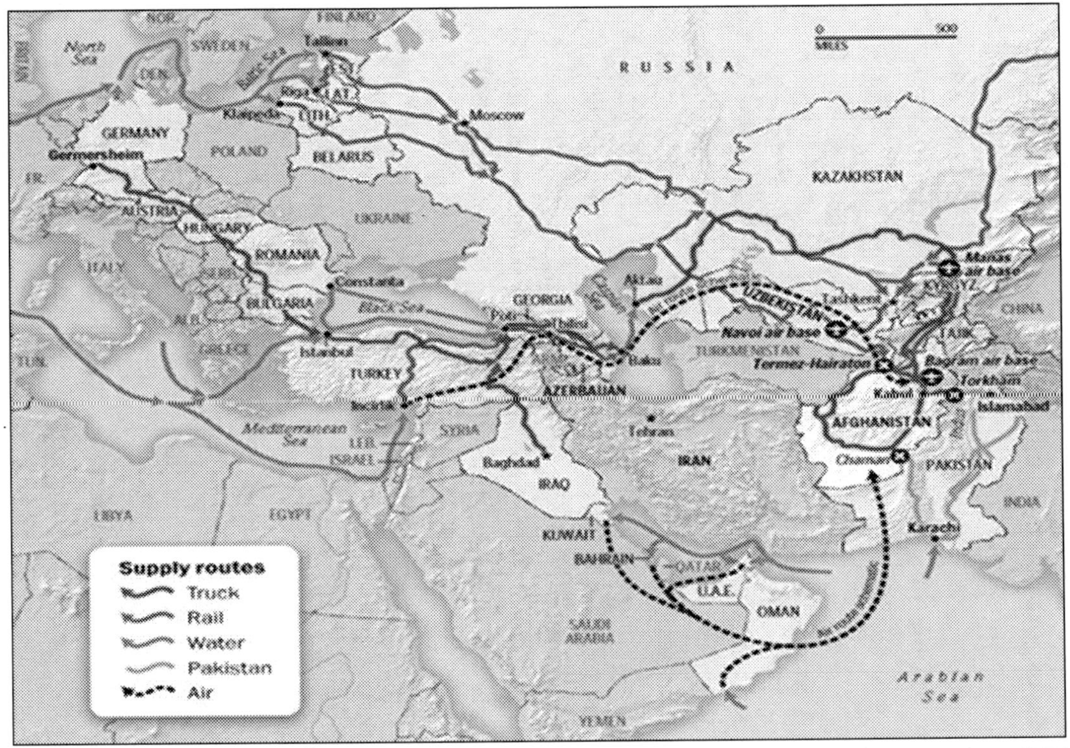

Source: http://www.washingtonpost.com/national/national-security/a-logistics-mira-cle/2011/07/02/AGZDwnvH_graphic.html

Nonetheless, Central Asian countries are still trying to balance the influence of Russia and China through engagement with United States.[13] United States will ensure its ability to influence events in the wider Central Asian region, control worsening insurgencies and the growth of radical forces as well as maintain pressure on Russia, China, Iran and Pakistan in the region.

Turkey-Central Asia

Main factor that stipulated the intense Turkish engagement with the Central Asian countries was ethnic ties of Turkey with Kazakhstan, Turkmenistan, Uzbekistan and Kyrgyzstan is the Turkic speaking population. Turkey's policies in Central Asia from the end of 1980s can be classified into three periods. Between 1989 and 1991, Turkey mainly pursued a Moscow-centric policy in its relations with the Central Asian states. In December 1991, the new period of Turkey-Central Asia relations started being called as "euphoria" period and lasted till 1993. Since 1993, serious disappointment and resentment followed from both the sides, which marked the beginning of a period classified as "from euphoria to despair", which lasted till 1995. Ankara expected that the Central Asian states would naturally accept Turkey as an "elder brother" while the Central Asian states viewed relations with Turkey as a tool for strengthening independence and achieving wider international recognition.[14]

Central Asian countries expected from Turkey tangible economic support and credits for saving their crumpling economies, while Turkey was not economically and politically ready to meet all the demands of Central Asian states. Turkish EXIMBANK credits, which were initially positively accepted by the Central Asian countries, later (due to the high interest rates) were declined and problems emerged for paying those rates. Several issues coming from internal politics of Turkey—like joining European Union and changes in strategic thinking in Turkey about its foreign policy—paved way for declining Turkey-Central Asia relations. Ankara changed its strategy in the region from *euphoric* and *romantic policies* of 'Turkish unity' and Turkey's natural leadership to more pragmatic and economically grounded strategies for establishment of *"pragmatic and practical relations"*, focusing on equal partner treatment and mutual respect strategies which continue till date.[15]

Iran-Central Asia

Iran, geographically proximate to the Central Asian states and directly bordered with the region, enjoyed historical/cultural ties. Independence of the Central Asian states also meant opening up the region for Iran's economic activity to ease international isolation and the impact of economic sanctions. Iran expressed concern about the rapid progress of Turkey in Central Asia.[16] Iran had serious disadvantage as Islamic identity of its ruling regime was unacceptable to Central Asian states. Iran supported several religious foundations in the region and attempted to contribute Islamic revival in Central Asia. Iran's relations with religious groups in Central Asia remained low. Iran emphasised on "regionalism" for intensifying relations with the Central Asian states through the regional frameworks like Economic Cooperation Organisation (ECO), Organisation of Islamic Conference (OIC), and SCO.[17]

Tehran developed close relations with Tajikistan, which shares the same ethnic and linguistic background with Iran. Iran gives special importance to Turkmenistan (borders with Iran), and realised several regional projects like gas pipelines and railway constructions.[18] Kazakhstan is relatively important partner for Iran. Kyrgyzstan, with its geographic location and lack of economic strength, largely remained out of Tehran's focus. Uzbekistan remains the most skeptical Central Asian state about Tehran's intentions in the region and reluctant to develop good neighbourly relations with Iran.[19] There are several issues—Iran's aggressive stance in the dispute around division of the Caspian Sea, nuclear ambitions of Tehran, religious identity of the Mullah Regime and US sanctions towards Iran and towards companies working with Iran—that negatively affect willingness in Central Asia to strengthen engagement with Iran and hampers development and bilateral relations.

India-Central Asia

In the early 1990s, India lagged behind other regional actors in Central Asia as India had just embarked on a policy of economic reforms, and it was in no position to exploit trade and investment opportunities with these new republics.[20] Moreover, direct transportation routes linking India and Central Asia, which could allow trade and other exchanges, were restricted by war in Afghanistan and unwillingness of Pakistan to allow rise of India-Central Asia trade relations as well as formidable geographical barrier such as the high-altitude Himalayan range.[21] Now, India declared "Connects Central Asia" policy as one of the priority foreign policy goals, and has shown insistence in its efforts—particularly India's economic growth—has facilitated these attempts.[22] Currently, India has considerable economic and security interests, as well as geopolitical considerations that allowed India for increased engagement with the Central Asian countries.

Conclusion

In Central Asia, almost all important global and regional players like Russia, China, United States, Turkey, Iran and India have certain interests. End of Soviet rule in Central Asia also brought about new opportunities and challenges for regional powers. However, three main players—Russia, China and United States—are having significant impact on these five Central Asian Republics. Russia continues to influence and define the course of many processes in Central Asia; in recent period, it has been observed that the activities of China in Central Asia have increased considerably. China started engaging both politically and economically in reasonably stronger way in Central Asia. While the regional countries, due to the world financial slowdown, are not able to economically make any impact on the region, China taking advantage of the situation is gradually but steadily rising its influence in Central Asia. Today, China is considered one of the most powerful geopolitical players in Central Asian region. Although the Central Asian countries welcome engaging China to balance the influence of Russia and United States,

China is also considered as the greater long-term threat by the Central Asian states. The United States, even after reducing its attention considerably in the region, will nonetheless try to maintain its strong position in Central Asian countries—both for issues related to Afghanistan and also for balancing Russia and China, and other regional powers in Central Asia.

India is determined to maintain a strong position in Central Asia; India needs comprehensive and future-oriented regional strategy towards the region. India and Central Asian states are trying to cooperate closely in trade and economic sector, in infrastructure etc. In order to eliminate the disadvantage on lack of connectivity, both India and the Central Asian states are now trying to be part of an extended trade network through the North–South transport corridor. India and Central Asian states are closely working with each other on the security sectors too, as the three CAR states bordering Afghanistan, i.e. Uzbekistan, Tajikistan and Turkmenistan, can curb security threats emanating from Afghanistan. There has been an articulated policy of India to integrate Central Asia with India, and consider an observer status for the CARs in SAARC forum. India's membership in the Economic Cooperation Organisation (ECO) can also strengthen India's economic relationship with the Central Asian states and could lead the relationship further, creating a meaningful partnership. There is also a need to look for ways to increase people-to-people contacts and step-up information sharing, which are now being considered seriously by the Indian side under the "Look Central Asia" policy. However, there is a need to place these realisations on the fast track.

END NOTES

1. Garimov Azad & Ibrahimov Rovshan, "Geopolitical Competition in the Central Asia: The Dynamics of Relations with Azerbaijan", Sam Comments, Volume IX, August, 2013, pp-7-8
2. ILgar Valizada, Центральная Азияи Южный Кавказ: интеграц, ионныепроцессы в сердце Евразии, Baku, 2010, p.6.
3. CIA World Factbook, available at https://www.cia.gov/library/publications/the-world-factbook.

4. Aida Kasymalieva, Erica Marat, "Kyrgyz and Tajik Migrants in Moscow", "Eurasia Daily Monitor", Volume, 9, Issue, 19, at http://www.jamestown.org/programs/edm/ single/?tx
5. Edward C. Chow and Leigh E. Hendrix, "Central Asia's Pipelines: Field of Dreams and Reality", the National Bureau of Asian Research, Special Report #23, September, 2010, p. 32
6. Stephen Aris, "Managing Central Asia: Russia's Approach", Swiss Federal University of Zurich, available at http://www.isn.ethz.ch/isn/Digital-Library/Articles/Special-Feature/Detail/?lng=en&id=160464&contextid774=160464&contextid775=160462&tabid=1454180197, March 2013.
7. James Nixey, "The Long Goodbye: Waning Russian Influence in the South Caucasus and Central Asia, Chatham House Briefing Paper, June 2013
8. Hans-Inge Lango, "China's Westward Expansion into Central Asia", Hegemonicobsessions.com, at http://hegemonicobsessions.com/?p=183, February 2013
9. Zabikhulla Saipov, "China's Economic Strategies for Uzbekistan and Central Asia: Building Roads to Afghan Strategic Resources and Beyond", "Eurasia Daily Monitor", Volume 9, Issue 172, 2012, also available at http://www.jamestown.org/single/?no_cache=1&tx_ttnews%5Btt_news%5D=39873

   Also see Roman Muzalevski, "China-Kyrgyzstan-Uzbekistan Railway Scheme: Fears, Hopes and Prospects", *Eurasia Daily Monitor*, Volume 9, Issue 102, Jamestown Foundation, 2012, available at http://www.jamestown.org/single/?no_ cache=1&tx_ttnews%5Btt_news%5D=39434
10. Stephen Blank, "The US in Central Asia: Beyond Afghanistan?", March 8, 2013, also available at http://www.isn.ethz.ch/isn/Digital-Library/Articles/Specialfeature/Detail/?lng=en&id=161009&contextid774=161009&contextid775=16 1006&tabid=1454205962
11. Jeffrey Mankoff, "The United States and Central Asia after 2014", Center for Strategic and International Studies, also available at http://csis.org/files/publication/130122_Mankoff_USCentralAsia_Web.pdf
12. Joshua Kucera, "Great Game in Central Asia after Afghanistan", "The Diplomat", available at http://thediplomat.com/2013/03/27/the-great-game-in-central-asia-after-afghanistan/2/.
13. Joshua Kucera, "Russia Opposes US Military Donations to Central Asia", *Eurasianet*, available at http://www.eurasianet.org/node/65555.
14. Heinz Kramer, "Will Central Asia Become Turkey's Sphere Of Influence", "Center for Strategic Studies of Turkey, available at http:/

/sam.gov.tr/wp-content/uploads/2012/01/8.-WILL-CENTRAL-ASIA-BECOME-TURKEYS-SPHERE-OF-INFLUENCE.pdf

15. Ceren Kumova, "Turkey commits heart and soul to Central Asia, just not strongly enough", "Today's Zaman", available at http://www.todayszaman.com/news-266876-turkey-commits-heart-and-soul-to-central-asia-just-not-strongly-enough.html
16. Svante E. Cornell, "Regional Politics in Central Asia: the Changing Roles of Iran, Turkey, Pakistan and China", in India and Central Asia: Building Linkages in an Age of Turbulence, Sapra Foundation, 2003, p. 4, also available at http://www.silkroadstudies.org/pub/030720Sapra.pdf
17. Arzu Naghiyev, "Central Asia as Iran's Savior", "Trend", available at http://en.trend.az/news/politics/2083404.html
18. Brenton Clark, "Persian Games: Iran's strategic foothold in Tajikistan", Open-democracy.net, available at http://www.opendemocracy.net/od-russia/brenton-clark/persian-games-iran%E2%80%99s-strategic-foothold-in-tajikistan.
19. Sebastien Peyrouse and Sadykzhan Ibraimov, "Iran's Central Asia Temptations, Current Trends in Islamist Ideology", Vol. 10, available at http://www.currenttrends.org/research/detail/irans-central-asia-temptations.
20. Sachdeva Gulshan, "India's Objectives in Central Asia", School of International Studies, Jawaharlal Nehru University, available at http://uschinacenter.as.nyu.edu/docs/IO/23889/Sachdeva_Abs.pdf
21. Roman Muzalevsky, "India's 'Connect Central Asia' Policy Seeks to Compensate for Lost Time", "Eurasia Daily Monitor", Volume 9, Issue 176, available at http://www.jamestown.org/single/?no_cache=1&tx_ttnews%5Btt_news%5D=39891
22. "Regional-Economic-Cooperation-Creates-the-TAPI-Pipeline", available at http://www.economywatch.com/features/Regional-Economic-Cooperation-Creates-the-TAPI- Pipeline1204.html.

Chapter 5

India-Kyrgyzstan Relations

Reena Pandey

Introduction

In the post-Cold War scenario, the year 1991 was a defining moment in the history of India's foreign and foreign economic policies. At one end was the collapse and disintegration of the USSR, and on the other was the acceleration of the process of globalisation. One of the most pronounced shifts in foreign policy was the "Look East" policy initiated in 1991. Another strong policy shift was the decision to open India's doors for foreign investments and to deregulate its economy and be part and parcel of the global economy. Several other important steps were taken over the next two decades, and these included strategic partnerships with USA, China, Russia and the EU. India also forged some important regional links through BRICS, IBSA etc. The success of the "Look East" policy led to further policy shifts. There is a focus on South Asia as our immediate neighbourhood remains crucially vital to our national interests, but we also turned our attention to closer relations with Africa. India's growing economy, the surging aspirations of 1.25 billion people, the unprecedented flux in the international order and national interests makes India look not just East but also North, South and West within its extended neighbourhood and beyond. The shift in economic power from the West to the East and to the rest underlines India's increasing emphasis on extended neighbourhood in its foreign policy practice and projection.

The last two decades saw India's economy grow and along with it, its hunger for hydrocarbons. This brought India closer to the energy-rich West Asia and Central Asia. There was a reshaping of India's security and strategic imperatives. Now let us look at India's burgeoning engagement with Central Asia, a region suffused with centuries–old cultural ties and friendly relations. With the threats to security in and around Afghanistan, this region has moved closer to the center of the global strategic canvas. Following the entry of Afghanistan into SAARC, Central Asia is now contiguous to South Asia. It provides us opportunities for greater political, economic and security engagement with the region. Its strategic importance stems not just from its geographical proximity but also from the fact that three of the five Central Asian countries have land frontiers with Afghanistan, and hence face common geo-strategic challenges. The turmoil in Afghanistan brought geo-strategic threats to the threshold of South and Central Asia. All the regional players have become stakeholders in the stability of Afghanistan.

The last two decades have been a period of intense political engagement and constant search for newer ways of economic engagement. Now there is no competition with the powers in the region and our relationships with Central Asia are based on a unique model of political, economic, strategic, and cultural, development partnership and multilateral elements. All the regional players are now interested in the development of the region and to ensure that fundamentalism and extremism do not find place in the region. Energy security is also a crucial driver of India's relationship with ambitious projects like TAPI on the table. A more pro-active phase of policy to engage Central Asia was publicly articulated in Bishkek in June 2012, called the "Connect Central Asia" policy. The elements of this policy included exchange of high level visits, strengthening of strategic and security co-operation, stepping up multilateral engagements, entering into comprehensive economic engagement, fostering innovative solutions in connectivity and deepening development partnerships.

An important highlight of India's relations with Central Asia is Prime Minister Modi's visit to the five Central Asian Republics in July 2015. The visit, apart from focusing on energy, trade and connectivity also sought to strengthen cultural ties between the two regions and deepen co-operation in climate change and counter terrorism. Looking back at the India-Kyrgyzstan bilateral relations, it was a momentous period for the Kyrgyz people when they emerged as an independent nation in the early 1990s, and two decades later became the only country in the region to adopt a parliamentary system of democracy. The two countries share warm political and cultural relations. The interactions between India and Kyrgyzstan go back to the time of the Sakas or the Scythians. Apart from trade along the fabled Silk Route, religion, particularly Buddhism, and philosophy were other influences. Archaeological discoveries point to several links between ancient towns and institutions of learning. History is replete with these linkages between the people of Central Asia and India. On the political front, the two countries have had exchanges of high level visits. The Kyrgyz leadership welcomes the ongoing peace process between India and Pakistan, supports India's bid for a permanent seat at the UNSC and welcomes India's membership in the Shanghai Cooperation Organisation.

Both countries share common concerns on threats of terrorism, extremism and drug trafficking. Both sides have signed several framework agreements, including on culture, trade and economic cooperation, civil aviation, investment promotion and protection, avoidance of double taxation, consular convention etc. Periodic foreign office consultations have facilitated greater understanding and provided a useful forum for exchange of views on bilateral and international issues. The seventh foreign office consultation was held in Bishkek in March 2015. The Inter-Governmental Commission on Trade, Economic, Scientific and Technological Cooperation held its

7th session in Delhi in March 2015. The highpoint of the bilateral relations was Prime Minister Modi's visit to Bishkek on 11-12th July, 2015. Bilateral discussion issues included trade, investment, defence cooperation, security, terrorism, culture and science and technology. Four agreements were signed on defence cooperation, on cultural cooperation memorandum of mutual understanding and cooperation in the field of elections, MOU between Kyrgyz Ministry of Economy and Bureau of Standards on cooperation in the sphere of standards. There was stress on cooperation in agriculture too. Around 60% of the population on both sides relies on agriculture. The Kyrgyz farmers also specialise in organic cultivation. India will focus on broadening development assistance-based ties to include greater sharing of Indian technical expertise in greenhouse technology, micro-irrigation, water conservation and enhancing agricultural productivity. Soon after the PM's visit, as an immediate follow-up process, a workshop on agriculture cooperation was held in Bishkek in July 2015 by the Technical Working Group. Projects have been identified and more discussions will take place. The Agriculture Ministry is to send a delegation to Kyrgyzstan to explore concrete proposals to implement agreements. For enhancing trade between Indian and Central Asia, the Department of Commerce of India has established a Study Group to conclude Free Trade Agreement (FTA) with the Eurasian Economic Union (EEU). Kyrgyzstan has welcomed the possibility of the FTA with the EEU. During our PM's visit to Kyrgyzstan, both sides had noted that the current level of economic, trade and investment linkages between India and Kyrgyzstan are below potential and there was need for concerted efforts to enhance the economic context of the bilateral partnership. An aforementioned impediment to bilateral trade with the Eurasian region is the absence of viable surface connectivity. There is much awareness regarding this problem on both sides, and India has made several efforts to increase road, rail, air and sea connectivity.

Many discussions with Civil Aviation authorities by Ministry of External Affairs (MEA) led to all the Central Asian countries being given rights to operate flights to India three years ago. For last one year, Kyrgyz Air Manas is operating two flights per week. This will have a positive effect on business and tourism. The report mentions that in 2014, the Kyrgyz Embassy issued 200 visas; in 2015 the number rose to 2000 visas. In Bishkek, Indian Embassy informed that there was a 25% increase in tourist visas. Flying time between Delhi and Bishkek is less than that between Delhi and destinations in South India. With regard to surface connectivity, we are making all the efforts to streamline further the International North- South Transport Corridor and improve access to and within the region. Two years ago, we reinvigorated meetings regarding the corridor. Last year, the Coordination Council and Expert Level Meetings were held in New Delhi. In January 2015, we supported a meeting of all stakeholders in Mumbai. In December 2015, business-to-business interaction on the corridor was held in Mumbai. On ground, the Corridor is working but it is not popular due to cumbersome customs clearances. There is a recommendation before the Coordination Council for one custom paper to be evolved so that transit is smooth. Most of our goods go through Iran and China. With the sanctions being lifted, Iran will see more traffic through Bander Abbas port. With regard to the Chabahar port, the Indian cabinet has approved building of dedicated berths. Then we also have the Trans-African routes.

During Prime Minister Modi's visit, great importance was attached to furthering economic cooperation. The Kyrgyz side invited Indian businesses to invest in their economy. On this front, there has been some positive movement, albeit of modest proportions. An Indian company has invested in gypsum mining, another in a hospitality venture in Issyk-Kul Lake and a third is on the anvil for a joint venture in pharmaceuticals in Kyrgyzstan. The direct air link, the development of other surface connectivity and investment by India in Kyrgyzstan would help in increasing bilateral trade—which in 2014-2015 amounted to US$ 40 million up from US$ 38 million in 2013-2014. About 97% of the trade is made up of exports from India.

There is very good prospect for tourism as well. Indian travellers are now looking for new places to visit and enjoy. Reaching Issyk-Kul from India would offer a new cost-effective holiday. In the first week of last month, the MEA had invited journalists from all Central Asian Countries for a one week stay in Delhi, Mumbai etc. Three journalists came from Kyrgyzstan; visas do not seem to be a problem now even for businessmen. With all these efforts, tourism should receive a boost. Further on the economic side, during PM's visit, the Indian side expressed its willingness to consider financing important socio-economic projects on mutually beneficial and acceptable terms; both sides will determine the conditions of financing. There is satisfaction on both sides over developing cooperation in sectors such as education and health. Over 1000 Kyrgyz professionals from a cross section of the Kyrgyz society have utilized the Indian Technical and Economic Cooperation (ITEC) Programme. In 2015, the training slots for Kyrgyz nationals have been increased from 80 to 100. The MEA financed India-Kyrgyz Centre for Information Technology (IT) established in the Bishkek University is functioning well. There is an agreement to work towards upgrading the centre , and setting up of similar centres in other major cities in Kyrgyzstan under Indian grant assistance is also on the horizon.

Health Care Sector

In the health sector, there are growing links, including regular visits by doctors from super specialty hospitals in India to Kyrgyzstan, visits of patients to India for medical treatment and complex surgery at affordable costs and international standards. In September 2014, India gifted a Computed Tomography Machine to the National Centre for Cardiology and Internal medicine. Kyrgyzstan is a popular destination for Indian medical students who number 3500 as against 2500 a year ago. Prime Minister Modi, during his visit to Bishkek, inaugurated the project to establish tele-medicine links between six highly specialised hospitals of India and six medical establishments in Kyrgyzstan. India also appreciates the support extended by Kyrgyzstan to the Kyrgyz-India Mountain Bio-Medical Research Centre. Both sides will continue research activity and the Kyrgyz side welcomed commencement of the second phase during the PM's visit.

Culture Sphere

India has strong cultural ties with Kyrgyzstan. There is a lot of cooperation in art, music, dance, theatre, cinema and other cultural manifestations. The Centre for Indian Studies set up in Osh State University in 1997 has been useful in providing exposure to Indian culture and civilisation to academicians. There have been several cultural exchanges between the two countries. Around 18-member Kyrgyz troupe was in India and they participated in the Surajkund Mela (exhibition-cum-fair) during February 2016. The Indian epic Mahabharat was staged in Bishkek during April 2016. Balika Vadhu, the popular Indian TV serial, was aired in Kyrgyz language on their TV channel I in 2015. Both countries have also expressed interest in joint study of common historical and cultural heritage. An India Study Centre was set up in the National Library of Kyrgyzstan in July 2014. The centre teaches Hindi, Yoga, classical music and dance.

Security Sphere

In the defence sector, the ties reflect a high level of mutual trust between the two countries. An agreement was signed between the two countries during the PM's visit on Cooperation in the Defence sector. Joint military exercises have taken place and the third exercise is scheduled to be held in India in March 2016. There is a decision to hold these exercises annually. The Indian government has provided medical equipment for the Kyrgyz Level II Field Hospital and established an IT centre at the Military Academy of the Armed Forces of the Kyrgyz government. There have been joint expeditions between the Armed Forces in mountain climbing and these exchanges will see continuation. The Indian government has also provided training for military officers in conducting Peace Keeping Courses. On terrorism, both sides share grave concerns over the rising trend of the extremism, radicalism and terrorism in the region, as well as in the world at large. Kyrgyzstan has a sizeable amount of ISIS members. The government has taken several steps in counteracting terrorism and in retaining the secular character of Kyrgyz society. Kyrgyz side also wants discussions with India on counter-terrorism through an institutionalised framework, and this is being considered.

Conclusion

Today, there are many positive trends in India-Kyrgyzstan bilateral relations. There are opportunities in gold mining and reverse innovations with Kyrgyzstan. Following Indian Prime Minister's visit, one can expect to see more developments in the coming years. The Government of India is viewing the region and bilateral relations with each Central Asian Republic as an important element of India's foreign policy. The government hopes to translate the close civilisational links that India has with the Central Asian countries into strong trade and economic relations, and better understanding among people from both the sides. It is India's firm belief that enhanced interaction and collaboration between India and Central Asia will contribute to stability and development in the entire Central and South Asian region.

REFERENCES

Information and data collected by author from the Ministry of External Affairs, Eurasian Division, South Block, New Delhi, During September 2016

Stobdan P. "Central Asia: Democracy Instability Strategic Game in Kyrgyzstan", Pentagon Press, 2014

Bakshi Jyotsna, ed. "Geopolitical Dynamics of India-Tajikistan Relations", Pentagon Press, 2015

Chapter 6

Afghan Factor in Security of Central Asian Republics

Raj Kumar Sharma

Introduction

Afghanistan is strategically located on the crossroads of South, Central and West Asia. It shares border with three Central Asian Republics (CARs)—Turkmenistan (804 km), Uzbekistan (144 km) and Tajikistan (1,357 km).[1] Around 40 to 50% of Afghanistan's population consists of Tajiks, Uzbeks and Turkmens, who live mainly in northern parts of the country. Along with Dari speaking Hazaras, the Tajiks and Uzbeks perceive themselves as natural rulers of northern Afghanistan and compete with Pashtuns for influence in these parts.[2] With shared borders and ethnicities, we can say that Afghanistan and CARs belong to same geopolitical space. In the historical context as well, northern Afghanistan and adjacent regions of Turkmenistan, Uzbekistan and Tajikistan have formed a common cultural and economic space as their riverine border could not act as a serious impediment to migration, trade, cultural and religious ideas and projection of political power.[3] The Bolshevik Revolution of 1917 brought Central Asia under the Soviet rule, which disturbed linkages between Afghanistan and Central Asia as the border between them was closed for the first time in their history. Under the Soviet rule in Central Asia, Turkmens, Uzbeks and Tajiks developed different cultural and political identities compared to their counterparts in Afghanistan. Afghanistan-Central Asia interaction resumed when Soviet Union invaded Afghanistan in 1979.[4] However, this failed to improve relations between Turkmens, Uzbeks and Tajiks on either side of Amu Darya. Due to continued conflict in Afghanistan, Central Asians have a negative image of the country.[5] After the US-NATO troop withdrawal from Afghanistan, CARs fear 'spillover' effects of the Afghan situation in the region. CARs (except Kazakhstan) are generally seen as victims of Afghan situation, not as actors with same capability like other neighbours.[6] The security threats for CARs that emanate from Afghanistan are non-traditional in nature, with terrorism being the topmost concern. Other threats include porous borders, drug trafficking and influx of Afghan refugees. The details of these threats are discussed in the following paragraphs.

Terrorism

The concerns of terrorism from Afghanistan to CARs are expressed as 'spillover' threat having two dimensions—direct and indirect. Taliban is often seen as a direct threat to CARs as some experts believe Taliban has transnational ambitions, and if it comes back to power by overthrowing the Afghan government, then it may not stop at Afghan borders. Indirectly, Taliban provides safe havens for Central Asian terror groups like Islamic Movement of Uzbekistan (IMU), which could target the CARs from their sanctuaries in Afghanistan.

Is Taliban a Threat to Central Asia?

The total number of Central Asian fighters present in Afghanistan and Pakistan can be between 2,000 and 3,000.[7] Taliban has provided safe havens to Central Asian terrorist groups who assist it in its fight against the Western forces and Afghan National Security Forces (ANSF). This has given rise to the speculation that Taliban is likely to expand to Central Asia. In mid 1990s, Russia (the primary security provider in Central Asia) saw Taliban as a threat not only to Central Asian Muslims, but also to a large Muslim population with in its own territory. After assuming power in Kabul, Taliban had directly challenged Russia by recognising Chechnya's independence from Russian Federation in 2000.[8] Alexander Lebed, secretary of Russian National Security Council in 1996, said after the fall of Kabul that route to Bukhara laid open for Taliban to march into heart of Russia.[9] Taliban's advance in northern Afghanistan posed threat to Central Asia's stability, which prompted Russia to support 'Northern Alliance' along with Iran and India.[10] In contemporary context, similar developments are taking place since Taliban is surging in Afghanistan while the battle is being extended to northern Afghanistan again. Earlier, northern Afghanistan served as a buffer between CARs and Afghan battle zones in south of the country.[11] However, erosion of this buffer due to a surging Taliban is causing 'domino effect' concerns for CARs. Although there has been a continuous debate over 'Talibanisation' of CARs, yet most of the scholars agree that Taliban has no direct interest in Central Asia. Experts like Alexei Malashenko, security analyst at Carnegie, Moscow, journalist Joshua Kucera and Central Asia analyst Jozef Lang believe that Taliban does not pose a direct threat to CARs. Malashenko sees Taliban s being too occupied in domestic affairs to concentrate on Central Asia.[12] Joshua Kucera believes real threats to Central Asia emanate from their internal problems, not from Taliban[13] while Jozef Lang has pointed out that Central Asia has never been an area of interest for the Taliban, which is a Pashtun movement.[14] Alexander Zelitchenko, director of the Central Asia Centre for Drug Policy in Bishkek, has also echoed similar thoughts saying that Taliban is unlikely to target Central Asia as they have never claimed territory held by others.[15] Even the deceased leader of Taliban, Mullah Akhtar Mansour, is earlier reported to have assured CARs that Taliban is not a threat to them and they should not see Taliban as an enemy.[16] There seems a strategic shift in

Russian views about Taliban, as it now sees the Islamic State offshoot in Afghanistan as a bigger threat compared to Taliban.

Afghanistan as a Safe Haven for Central Asian Terror Groups

Afghanistan has played an ideological role in the rise of extremism in CARs, mainly in Uzbekistan where Tahir Yuldashev and Juma Namangani took advantage of socio-economic disorganisation and established *Adolat* (Justice in Uzbek) in 1991. The group was based on radical Salafist ideology and operated from Namangan in Fergana Valley, where it assumed governance responsibility by imposing Sharia laws.[17] It is important to emphasise here that Namangani was a paratrooper in the Soviet Army who served in Soviet-Afghan war. His close friends claim that Namangani's experiences in this war transformed him into a 'born again Muslim'.[18] This is in reference to his experiences with Pakistan created and US-Saudi backed Mujahidin in Afghanistan to fight the Soviet Army during the decade-long Soviet-Afghan war.[2] President of Uzbekistan, Islam Karimov, resorted to repression and launched a systemic crackdown against *Adolat*. This sent the leaders of the movement into exile in their training camps in Tajikistan and Afghanistan, making it more structured overseas than in Uzbekistan.[19] In Tajikistan, *Adolat* fought alongside Islamic Renaissance Party (IRP) during the civil war in the 'Namangani Battalion' and developed close contacts with jihadists in Pakistan and Afghanistan.[20] However, isolated by IRP's political concessions in Tajikistan, *Adolat* renamed itself Islamic Movement of Uzbekistan (IMU) in 1998, with a declared objective to overthrow Islam Karimov's regime in Uzbekistan.[21]

IMU was able to carry out a number of terrorist attacks in Central Asia, like the Batken attacks in southern Kyrgyzstan in 1999, Tashkent explosions in February 1999 and Surkhandarya attacks in Uzbekistan in 2000.[22] Uzbekistan was concerned as IMU was using territory of other CARs to target it, and launched air strikes against IMU presence in Tajikistan and Kyrgyzstan without notifying either governments.[23] This showed that there was lack of coordinated response from CARs to deal with a common enemy, and this could have led to interstate conflict had Tajikistan and Kyrgyzstan taken strong exception to Uzbek actions. Meanwhile, Namangani left Tajikistan in November 1999 for Mazar-i-Sharif as Yuldashev had already struck a deal with the Taliban. The deal allowed IMU to use Afghanistan as a base to carry out attacks against Uzbekistan but in return, IMU had to fight for Taliban against Northern Alliance.[24] Once in Afghanistan, IMU developed links with al-Qaeda too, and Osama bin Laden is believed to have given USD 26 million to IMU in early 2000 for transport helicopters.[25] Amid growing resources and capability, the IMU changed its name to the Islamic Party of Turkestan in June 2001 and set ambitious agenda of creating an Islamic state in Central Asian region.[26] However, their plans could not take off as desired since the US launched its 'War on Terror' campaign in Afghanistan after the 9/11 terrorist strikes by al-Qaeda. US effort was welcomed by Russia and CARs as they had 'common' interest in checking terrorism in the region.

IMU was forced to shift its activities to South Waziristan in Pakistan under Taliban commander of the area, Maulvi Nazir and later shifted to other parts of Federally Administered Tribal Areas (FATA) in 2007.[27]

The US operations dismantled IMU leadership as Namangani was killed in 2001 while Yuldashev was killed in 2009. IMU also suffered a split in 2002, leading to birth of pro-al-Qaeda offshoot, Islamic Jihad Union, later named as Islamic Jihad Group (IJG).[28] It carried out attacks in Uzbekistan killing 47 people in 2004.[29] It was recently involved alongside Taliban in their Kunduz offensive in 2015.[30] On the other hand, IMU joined Pakistan Taliban and had claimed responsibility for carrying out Karachi airport attack in 2014. Ever since Pakistan military launched its Zarb-e-Azb operation against terrorists, many foreign terrorists, including those of IMU, have shifted to northern Afghanistan and Central Asia. This has shifted geography of Afghan war from southern to northern provinces like Kunduz, Badakhshan, Faryab and Takhar which share borders with CARs.[31] Even distant Kazakhstan has witnessed terrorist attacks which have linkages to Afghanistan. In 2011, attacks were carried out by a previously unknown group, Jund-al-Khilafah (Soldiers of the Caliphate) in Kazakh cities of Almaty, Atyrau and Taraz.[32] The authorities in Kazakhstan believe the group is hiding in areas on the Af-Pak border.[33]

The above analysis of radical elements in Central Asia can be categorised in three waves. In the first wave, the radical elements tried power sharing with local stakeholders (Tajikistan) while in second wave, they appealed to anti-regime and nationalistic sentiments (IMU). In the third wave, the radical elements are externally sponsored and their movement is supranational in character, not merely limited to Central Asia (Islamic State, al-Qaeda).[34] The Central Asian governments benefitted a great deal from the US 'War on Terror' operation. The US paid big amounts of money to CARs for using their facilities in its anti-terror operations, and its military presence made the region more secure. However, since the US-NATO presence has declined in Afghanistan, security concerns are again being expressed in CARs about the Afghan situation. According to Tokon Mamytov, a former deputy head of Kyrgyzstan's State Committee for National Security, the professional Central Asian militants from Afghanistan could return home and take over Fergana Valley in a week since our Army is not in good shape.[35]

Despite 'spillover' concerns, there is a general agreement among experts that such external threats are exaggerated by the Central Asian governments to deflect attention from more serious threats to the region which are internal in character.[36] It also allows them to undermine opposition forces and strengthen their hold on power. A case in point is Tajikistan where Islamic Renaissance Party of Tajikistan's (IRPT) has been branded as a terrorist group, and all its activities have been shut down in September 2015.[37] This is not to say that Central Asian terrorists based in Afghanistan and Afghan-Pakistan border do not pose a threat to CARs. However, terrorist groups like IMU pose a 'limited' threat to Central Asia which becomes a force multiplier when combined with problems like poverty, ethnic tensions, food insecurity, unemployment and state repression amid other issues. Even the capability of these terrorist groups to attack Central Asia is under scanner. There is lack of centralisation in such terrorist groups as their leadership has been dismantled. Fundamental groups have run out of steam and lack popular support in Central Asia, as the society in the region is more inclined towards Marxist-Leninist approach rather than Islamist outlook due to Communist influence.[38] In addition, the Sufi tradition of Islam that is prevalent in Central Asia is peaceful and inclusive, which largely negates influence of radical Islamic ideologies like Salafism and Wahabism.

Porous Borders and Drug Trafficking

Afghanistan shares porous borders with CARs marked by a terrain that includes plains, mountains and rivers. Such border not only facilitates movement of terrorists but also drug trafficking. Unlike Afghan-Turkmenistan and Afghan-Tajikistan border, the Afghan-Uzbekistan border is well guarded by the Uzbek authorities. Uzbekistan is strategically vital to Central Asian security. It not only borders Afghanistan but also four CARs. Radical elements can reach all CARs using Uzbekistan territory if its borders are not well guarded. Movement of IMU into Tajikistan and Kyrgyzstan via mountainous terrain that was not well guarded in the past highlights importance of effective border controls in CARs to check terrorism and drugs trafficking.[39] Afghanistan is the largest opium producer in the world, accounting for 80% of the global production. This opium is trafficked through Central Asia to Russia and Europe, and one of the key routes is called the 'Northern Route' through Turkmenistan, Uzbekistan and Tajikistan. Even the Northern Distribution Network established by NATO forces for logistics supply to its forces in Afghanistan is being used by drug traffickers.[40] Tajikistan, which shares the longest border among CARs with Afghanistan, witnesses annual smuggling of around 80 tons of heroin and 20 tons of opium through its territory to markets in Russia and Europe. Major portion of this flow takes place through the narrow Pyanj river that separates Afghan Badakhshan from Tajik

Badakhshan.[41] Things are no better in neighbouring Kyrgyzstan, where southern city of Osh in Fergana valley is also called 'drug capital' of Kyrgyzstan. Authorities seized over six tons of different kinds of drugs in Kyrgyzstan in 2012.[42] Things can be said to be even worse in Turkmenistan, where drug use has engulfed certain sections of military, mainly the units which serve on Afghan and Iran borders. The issue is so deep rooted that Turkmenistan has established a section for military personnel in the drug treatment centre run by the government.[43] Kazakhstan is of the view that opium trade is doing a lot of damage beyond Afghanistan's borders, and main focus of international assistance should be to deal with opium production in Afghanistan.[44] It is estimated that around 70% of Afghan opium is converted into heroine in Afghanistan itself. This conversion process requires high amount of acetic anhydride (nearly 1,500 tons) and 9,000 other chemicals. Afghanistan is incapable of locally producing acetic anhydride, which means they are brought in Afghanistan from other countries. It is possible that a part of this supply is trafficked through CARs which are unable to check it due to lack of intelligence and inadequately trained and equipped border guards.[45]

There are a number of problems faced by CARs due to drug trafficking. Use of opium in Central Asia is 0.8% of the adult population, which is double the world average. Criminal gangs and extremist organisations use drug trafficking to fund their activities, especially in the Fergana valley. Drug trafficking undermines legitimacy of state institutions as it creates corruption among various government bodies.[46] The increased use of injecting drugs is associated with rising number of HIV cases in Central Asia. The number of new cases diagnosed for HIV infections in the region has increased 14 times the figure in the year 2000 and ironically, half of them are the cases which inject drugs.[47] The efforts to check drug trafficking in Central Asia have been ineffective so far as the elites in Afghanistan and CARs are connected to huge profits in this illegal trade. There is lack of political will to check it while efforts to open legitimate cross border trade between Afghanistan and CARs have not taken place.[48]

Afghan Refugees in Central Asia

Tajik President Emomali Rahmon in 2010 had expressed concern over US-NATO withdrawal from Afghanistan; highlighting concerns over illegal migration in Central Asia from Afghanistan.[49] Intensification of Afghan war could trigger flow of refugees from Afghanistan to CARs. CARs had tough time dealing with refugee flow from Tajikistan during the Tajikistan Civil War in early years of their independence. The refugee issue is probably the only soft security matter in which Central Asian authorities want greater foreign involvement.[50] During the Afghan war in 1990s, the United Nations High Commissioner for Refugees (UNHCR) had come to the rescue of 10,000 Afghans stranded at the Afghan-Tajik border due to intense fighting in northern Afghanistan.[51] In Tajikistan, 97% of nearly 4,000 refugees and asylum-seekers are Afghans, which is also the biggest refugee population in the region.[52] Kazakhstan, too, could see influx of refugees who could use it as a transit to reach Europe via Belarus.[53] The concerns over influx of refugees from Afghanistan led to establishment of *Almaty Process* in 2011 aimed at addressing complex and mixed migration issues in Central Asia. Uzbekistan is not a member of the process while Afghanistan, Turkey, Azerbaijan and other four CARs are its members. The effort is supported by UNHCR and International Organisation for Migration (IOM).[54] Despite such efforts, the national refugee policies in Central Asia are inferior to international standards. The regional governments are too focused on transnational and cross border threats which hampers development of good refugee policy.[55] Any large wave of refugee influx from Afghanistan in economically weak countries like Tajikistan and Kyrgyzstan could also lead to local socio-economic discontent, which could prompt the governments to tighten their refugee policies.

Afghanistan and Central Asian Economic Security

The Central Asian economies are varied, having different characteristics Kyrgyzstan and Tajikistan are dependent on remittances, Turkmenistan and Kazakhstan depend on resource export (oil and gas) while Uzbek economy is a suboptimal combination of these two aspects.[56] In near future, Afghanistan could play an important role in economic security of the CARs as they are likely to be economically integrated. At the moment, Afghanistan and the CARs are 'marginal economic hinterlands' which are not mutually connected but oriented in different directions. Afghan economy is more oriented towards Pakistan, Iran and India while Russia and China dominate economy of CARs.[57] However, the US had shown interest in developing Afghanistan as a regional hub of energy and trade corridors, linking Central and South Asia, as manifest in Fredrick Starr's concept of 'Greater Central Asia'.[58] Consequently, the US has backed projects in this direction like Turkmenistan–Afghanistan–Pakistan–India Pipeline (TAPI) and Central Asia South Asia (CASA-1000) project to supply electricity to Afghanistan and Pakistan from Kyrgyzstan and Tajikistan. Such initiatives will lessen economic dependence of CARs on Russia and China. They will also lessen Tajikistan's economic dependence on Uzbekistan and Kazakhstan.[59] Landlocked CARs can also find a gateway to sea through Afghanistan. India recently signed a trilateral agreement with Iran and Afghanistan, where India will invest in Iran's Chabahar port to connect Afghanistan and Central Asia through Zaranj-Delaram-Chabahar route. However, these projects would come to fruition only if there is stability in Afghanistan.

Response from CARs

When the Taliban regime came to power in 1996 in Kabul, CARs severed their diplomatic relations with the Taliban government. Only Turkmen President Saparmurat Niyazov in Turkmenistan continued commercial relations with Kabul under his neutral foreign policy stance.[60] There has been no unified response from the CARs in response to Afghan situation, and they have followed different policies in dealing with the issue. Kazakhstan, Kyrgyzstan and Tajikistan have shown willingness to join multilateral forums to deal with the situation while Turkmenistan and Uzbekistan have pursued unilateral, non-aligned and even isolationist policies.[61] Uzbekistan competes with Kazakhstan for regional influence, and has been apprehensive about leaning too much on Russia in security matters. That is why, Tashkent gave up membership of Russian-led Collective Security Treaty Organisation (CSTO) in 2012. However, of late, President Karimov has endorsed Russian role in solving Afghan issues.[62] Turkmenistan follows a foreign policy marked by 'neutrality' and has not joined any security or economic initiative like Shanghai Cooperation Organisation (SCO), Eurasian Economic Union (EEU) or the CSTO. The only exception to this trend is 'Heart of Asia-Istanbul Process' regional dialogue started in 2011, where all CARs and Afghanistan are members to discuss political, economic and security issues related to Afghan issues.

Kazakhstan has focused on economic reconstruction of Afghanistan through its official development assistance (ODA) agency, kazAID.[63] President Nazarbayev has said that economic reconstruction of Afghanistan should be prioritised over democracy-building.[64] Kazakhstan has also proposed to institute a UN hub in Almaty where CARs can coordinate their efforts to aid Afghanistan.[65] Unlike Kazakhstan's economic focus, Uzbekistan has been highlighting the Afghan issue at different political platforms. President Karimov has been active at the United Nations, freely expressing his views on Afghanistan. It was due to Uzbekistan's efforts that Contact Group '6+2' (1997) and Contact Group '6+3' (2008) were established on Afghanistan.[66] Turkmenistan supplies electricity to Afghanistan and also provides educational and medical aid to Turkmen minority in Afghanistan.[67] Tajikistan and Kyrgyzstan have their own economic problems but are looking to export additional electricity to Afghanistan through CASA-1000 project. Kyrgyzstan in 2009 had proposed establishment of 'Bishkek Initiative' to host international conferences on Afghanistan and Central Asia.[68] However, the idea has not materialised yet. Tajikistan, too, has played instrumental role in instituting 'Dushanbe Four' in 2009 comprising Russia, Pakistan, Afghanistan and Tajikistan. The initiatives taken by CARs regarding Afghanistan have not been influential as some of them have not been instituted while these countries also lack financial and military means to effect a change in the Afghan problem. The CARs lack individual capacity to tackle security concerns like terrorism, and have depended on external powers for such concerns. These countries welcomed US presence in Afghanistan since it was also beneficial for them. Since the US presence has been scaled down, Russia is trying to strengthen its military hold in the Central Asian region. China has recently proposed to establish an anti-terrorism alliance with Afghanistan, Pakistan and Tajikistan, but it is surprising as it excludes Russia.

Conclusion

The Taliban may not pose a direct threat to CARs but terrorist groups like IMU do pose a direct threat to CARs. However, this constitutes a 'limited' threat to CARs, which becomes a force multiplier when combined with internal problems such as ethnic tensions, poverty, unemployment, repression by authorities, food insecurity etc. The governments in Central Asia are likely to use threat of terrorism to further undermine their opponents, particularly in Tajikistan and Uzbekistan. Drug trafficking could be said to be a bigger threat than terrorism, as it impacts a larger section of the society. It also leads to a weak state structure as it creates corruption and inefficiency among various government bodies. Afghanistan, if stabilized, could facilitate economic integration of Central and South Asia. Only Kazakhstan has been making an economic contribution to nation building processes in Afghanistan. Some initiatives mooted by the CARs regarding Afghanistan have not even started because they lack economic and military potential to make an impact in Afghanistan. This makes them dependent on external powers. Unified response from CARs to deal with threats from Afghanistan is unlikely, as they follow different paths in their foreign policies.

END NOTES

1. CIA World Factbook Data, available at https://www.cia.gov/library/publications/the-world-factbook/geos/af.html.
2. Martin Mccauley (2002), "Afghanistan and Central Asia: A Modern History", Oxon: Routledge.

3. Christian Bleuer and Said Reza Kazemi (2014), "Between Co-operation and Insulation Afghanistan's Relations with the Central Asian Republics", AAN Thematic Report 01/2014, available at https://www.afghanistan-analysts.org/wp-content/uploads/2014/06/20140608-Bleuer_Kazemi-Central_Asia.pdf.
4. Stratfor Analysis (2013), "Central Asia and Afghanistan: A Tumultuous History", September 24, available at https://www.stratfor.com/analysis/central-asia-and-afghanistan-tumultuous-history.
5. Bayram Balci and Didier Chaudet (2014), "Jihadism in Central Asia: A Credible Threat After the Western Withdrawal From Afghanistan?", Carnegie Endowment for International Peace, available at http://carnegieendowment.org/2014/08/13/jihadism-in-central-asia-credible-threat-after-western-withdrawal-from-afghanistan.
6. Marlene Laruelle et. al. (2013), "The Afghanistan Central Asia relationship: What role for the EU?", available at http://fride.org/descarga/EUCAM_WP13_Afghanistan.pdf.
7. Bayram Balci and Didier Chaudet op. cit.
8. The Taliban Formally Recognizes Chechnya, January 18, 2000, Jamestown Foundation, available at http://www.jamestown.org/single/?no_cache=1&tx_ttnews%5Btt_news%5D=11421#.Vy3Bd_lcSko.
9. Quoted in Lena Jonson (2004), "Vladimir Putin and Central Asia: The Shaping of Russian Foreign Policy", London: I B Tauris& Co. Ltd.
10. Hooman Peimani (2003), "Falling Terrorism and Rising Conflicts: The Afghan Contribution to Polarization and Confrontation in West and South Asia", Westport: Greenwood Press.
11. Stratfor Analysis 2013, op. cit.
12. Alexei Malashenko Quoted in Sergey Strokan and Vladimir Mikheev (2015), "Is there a Taliban-ISIS double threat to Russia and Central Asia?", Russia Beyond the Headlines, October 8, available at http://rbth.com/international/2015/10/08/is_there_a_taliban-isis_double_threat_to_russia_and_central_asi_49925.html.
13. Joshua Kucera Quoted in Bruce Pannier (2014), "Post-2014 Central Asia And Afghanistan", Radio Free Europe Radio Liberty, May 19, available at http://www.rferl.org/content/post-2014-central-asia-afghanistan/25390563.html.
14. Jozef Lang (2014), "Nervousness in Central Asia after the Taliban seize Kunduz", October 14, available at http://www.osw.waw.pl/en/publikacje/analyses/2015-10-14/nervousness-central-asia-after-taliban-seize-kunduz.
15. Alexander Zelitchenko Quoted in Saule Mukhametrakhimova (2013), "Central Asia at Risk From Post-2014 Afghanistan", available at

https://iwpr.net/global-voices/central-asia-risk-from-post-2014-afghanistan.

16. Lailuma Noori (2015), "Extremist movements in north a threat to Central Asia, experts", The Kabul Times, October 11, available at http://thekabultimes.gov.af/index.php/opinions/politics/8335-extremist-movements-in-north-a-threat-to-central-asia-experts.html.
17. Mathieu Guidère (2012), "Historical Dictionary of Islamic Fundamentalism", Maryland: Scarecrow Press Inc.
18. Ahmed Rashid (2002), "They're Only Sleeping: Why militant Islamicists in Central Asia aren't going to go away", January 14, The New Yorker, available at http://www.newyorker.com/magazine/2002/01/14/theyre-only-sleeping.
19. Bayram Balci and Didier Chaudet op. cit.
20. Zumrat Salmorbekova and Galina Yemelianova (2010), "Islam and Islamism in Ferghana Valley", in Galina Yemelianova (ed), *Radical Islam in the Former Soviet Union*, Oxon: Routledge.
21. Ehsan Ahrari (2007), "Countering Ideological Support – The Case of Fergana Valley", in Anne Aldis and Graeme Herd (eds.), *The Ideological War on Terror: Worldwide Strategies For Counter-Terrorism*, Oxon: Routledge.
22. Akram Umarov (2014), "The relations of the Central Asian countries and Afghanistan in the new century", *Defence Journal*, August 2014, Vol. 18 Issue 1.
23. Matthew Stein (2012), "Uzbekistan's View of Security in Afghanistan After 2014", *Military Review*, May-June 2012.
24. Ahmed Rashid op. cit.
25. Ibid.
26. Islamic Movement of Uzbekistan (IMU), Islamic Party of Turkestan Profile available at http://www.globalsecurity.org/military/world/para/imu.htm.
27. Jacob Zenn (2012), "The Indigenization of the Islamic Movement of Uzbekistan", Jamestown Foundation, Terrorism Monitor Volume: 10 Issue: 2, available at http://www.jamestown.org/single/?tx_ttnews%5Btt_news%5D=38931&no_cache=1#.VymbCNR97 Gh.
28. Cerwyn Moore (2010), "The Rise and Fall of the Islamic Jihad Union: What Next for Uzbek Terror Networks?", Jamestown Foundation, Publication: Terrorism Monitor Volume: 8 Issue: 14, available at http://www.jamestown.org/programs/tm/single/?tx_ttnews%5Btt_news%5D=36251&cHash=05af7 9606d#.Vymm4dR97Gg.
29. Jim Nichol (2006), "Central Asia: Regional Developments and Implications for U.S. Interests", CRS Report for Congress, available at http://fpc.state.gov/documents/organization/68821.pdf.

30. Bill Roggio and Thomas Joscelyn (2015), "Central Asian groups split over leadership of global jihad", *The Long War Journal*, August 24, available at http://www.longwarjournal.org/archives/2015/08/central-asian-groups-split-over-leadership-of-global-jihad.php.
31. Tamim Asey (2015), "Central Asia's Stake in Afghanistan's War," The Diplomat, July 29, available at http://thediplomat.com/2015/07/central-asias-stake-in-afghanistans-war/.
32. Uwe Halbach (2013), "Afghanistan 2014: Shadows over Central Asia?", Security and Human Rights 24, 137-148.
33. Robin Paxton (2011), "Islamist militant kills seven in attack in Kazakh city", *Reuters*, November 12, available at http://www.reuters.com/article/us-kazakhstan-blast-idUSTRE7AB08220111112.
34. Rouben Azizian (2005), "Islamic Radicalism in Kazakhstan and Kyrgyzstan: Implications for the Global War on Terrorism", available at kms2.isn.ethz.ch/serviceengine/Files/RESSpecNet/44044/.../10.pdf.
35. Yaroslav Trofimov (2015), "Central Asia Fears Afghan Contagion", *The Wall Street Journal*, December 17, available at http://www.wsj.com/articles/central-asia-fears-afghan-contagion-1450366559.
36. Ulla Schmidt (2015), "Transition in Afghanistan: Implications for Central Asia", NATO Special Report, October 11, available at http://www.nato-pa.int/default.asp?SHORTCUT=3773.
37. Shuttered Tajik Islamic Party Branded As Terrorist Group, Radio Free Europe Radio Liberty, September 29, 2015, available at http://www.rferl.org/content/tajikistan-islamic-party-terrorist-organization/27277385.html.
38. Bayram Balci and Didier Chaudet op. cit.
39. Matthew Stein op. cit.
40. Joshua Kucera (2013), "UN: NDN An Express Train For Afghan Drug Traffickers", April 24, available at http://www.eurasianet.org/node/66871.
41. Yaroslav Trofimov (2012), "Afghan Drug Trade Sends Tremors", *The Wall Street Journal*, August 3, available at http://www.wsj.com/articles/SB10000872396390443545504577563414182938548.
42. Central Asia's 'Drug Capital' Fights to Stem Tide of Narcotics, January 4, 2013, available at http://www.rferl.org/content/osh-is-awash-in-drugs/24815565.html.
43. Paul Goble (2015), "Threatened From Afghanistan, Turkmenistan Faces Serious Military Manning Shortfalls", The Jamestown Foundation, March 2, available at http://jamestownfoundation.blogspot.in/2015/03/threatened-from-afghanistan.html.
44. Yerzhan Kazykhanov (2012), "Stabilizing Afghanistan: The View from Kazakhstan", May 18, available at http://www.realclearworld.com/

articles/2012/05/18/stabilizing_afghanistan_the_view_from_kazakhstan.html

45. Securing Central Asia's Borders with Afghanistan, Outline Action Plan of UNODC, 2007, available at https://www.unodc.org/documents/regional/central-asia/Microsoft%20Word%20-%20yellow_paper__no%20maps_16.09.17.pdf.
46. Ulla Schmidt op. cit.
47. Central Asia in the spotlight: growing HIV epidemic among people who inject drugs (2012), WHO Report, available at http://www.euro.who.int/en/media-centre/sections/press-releases/2012/06/central-asia-in-the-spotlight-growing-hiv-epidemic-among-people-who-inject-drugs
48. Deirdre Tynan Quoted in Gabriel Domínguez (2015), "Why Central Asia is increasingly worried about Afghanistan", November 4, available at http://www.dw.com/en/why-central-asia-is-increasingly-worried-about-afghanistan/a-18826223.
49. Tajikistan concerned over decision to withdraw anti-terrorist coalition forces from Afghanistan, December 3, 2010, RIA Novosti, available at http://sputniknews.com/world/20101203/161608664.html.
50. Marlene Laruelle et. al. op. cit.
51. Central Asia Regional Overview, UNHCR Global Report 2000, available at http://www.unhcr.org/cgi-bin/texis/vtx/home/opendocPDFViewer.html?docid=3e23eb617&query=afghans.
52. 2015 UNHCR subregional operations profile - Central Asia, UNHCR, available at http://www.unhcr.org/pages/49e45afd6.html.
53. Jos Boonstra et. al. (2014), "The Impact of the 2014 ISAF Forces' Withdrawal From Afghanistan on the Central Asian Region", Directorate-General For External Policies Of The Union, European Union Study, available at https://www.gwu.edu/~ieresgwu/assets/docs/ISAF_2014.pdf.
54. Almaty Process on Refugee Protection and International Migration, available at https://www.iom.int/sites/default/files/our_work/ICP/RCP/2015/2015-Global-RCP-Almaty-Process-Presentation.pdf.
55. 2015 UNHCR op. cit.
56. Andrew C. Kuchins and Thomas M. Sanderson (2010), "The Northern Distribution Network and Afghanistan: Geopolitical Challenges and Opportunities", available at http://csis.org/files/publication/091229_Kuchins_NDNandAfghan_Web.pdf.
57. Christian Bleuer and Said Reza Kazemi op. cit.
58. S. Frederick Starr (2005), "A 'Greater Central Asia Partnership' for Afghanistan and Its Neighbors", Silk Road Paper, available at http://www.silkroadstudies.org/resources/pdf/SilkRoadPapers/2005_starr_a-greater-central-asia-partnership.pdf.

59. Nargis Kassenova (2014), "Relations between Afghanistan and Central Asian states after 2014: Incentives, Constraints and Prospects", SIPRI, available at http://books.sipri.org/files/misc/SIPRI14wcaNK.pdf.
60. Marlene Laruelle et. al., op. cit.
61. Ulla Schmidt op. cit.
62. Uzbek president: Afghanistan's problems cannot be solved without Russia, April 26, 2016, TASS, available at http://tass.ru/en/world/872458.
63. Christian Bleuer and Said Reza Kazemi op. cit.
64. Nazarbayev: "economy first, then politics", January 15, 2010, available at http://www.euronews.com/2010/01/15/nazarbayev-economy-first-then-politics/
65. Nadezhda Khamitova (2013), "Efforts to Create UN Regional Diplomacy Hub in Almaty Continue", *The Astana Times*, May 29, available at http://astanatimes.com/2013/05/efforts-to-create-un-regional-diplomacy-hub-in-almaty-continue/.
66. Islam Karimov: Uzbek people need peace and tranquillity, August 8, 2013, available at http://politics.uzreport.uz/news_e_107671.html.
67. Marlene Laruelle et. al., op. cit.
68. Speech by Kyrgyz PM Igor Chudinov at the UN (2009), available at http://www.un.org/en/ga/64/generaldebate/KG.shtml.

Conclusion
India and the Central Asian States

Nivedita Das Kundu

The United Services Institution of India (USI) and International Ataturk Alatoo University (IAAU), under the scope of a MoU, conducted the joint research projects that have dominated the discourse in India as well as in the Central Asian states. Under its ambit, four Indian and two Kyrgyz scholars conducted the study. The outcome of the joint research is produced in one volume, giving two separate perspectives. Beyond the granularities of this contemporary project, the joint research also obliquely brought the overall nature of this significant bilateral relation.

This volume highlighted that Central Asia, as a collective geographical entity, had been part of the Soviet Union for about a century and a half before the Soviet Union unravelled. The break-up led to the emergence of 15 independent states in 1991. These newly independent states brought new challenges and opportunities for India to broaden its bilateral and multilateral relationships with all the five Central Asian states. Since the Soviet period, India had close relationship with all the former Soviet states, including five Central Asian countries. Although India's close cooperation with the Soviet Union was indeed an advantage for developing relationship with the post-Soviet newly independent states of Central Asia, in the changed situation, there was a need to shift its focus from the larger canvas of the Soviet Union to a smaller canvas to renew and build close ties with each of these five new Republics.

Central Asia had been historically a zone of India's civilisational influence. Historically, India had close contacts with five Central Asian states of Kazakhstan, Kyrgyzstan, Uzbekistan, Tajikistan and Turkmenistan. Interactions between India and Central Asian states had begun since the time of the ancient Silk Route days. Intense contacts took place when Indian traders visited Fergana valley to trade along the Silk Route, and that continued for many years. Central Asia also acquired philosophical ideas and knowledge through the Silk Route connections. The influence of Buddhism flowed from India to Central Asia and beyond through the Silk Route linkages.

History is full of friendly interactions among Indians and the Central Asians through movement of people, goods and ideas, including spiritual interface that were not without advantage to common heritage. The five Central Asian countries are treated as a single geopolitical area. This strategically-located, resource-rich region came into prominence mainly after the collapse of the Soviet Union, when these states became independent sovereign states. Today, Central Asia is occupying an increasingly crucial place in international power politics. These five nations are at varying stages of political and economic development. Some are vibrant democracies, whereas others are still following centralised regimes.

In this volume, the authors, in their respective chapters, also discuss that Central Asian countries' location between, Russia, China, Iran, and Afghanistan makes the region a focal point for foreign powers as well as, for the potential conflict between them. It can thus be said that the region is at the center of a new 'Great Game.' However, unlike the Great Game of the 19th century which was played out between the British Empire and the Czarist Russia, the post-Cold War Great Game in Central Asia involves not only states, but also non-state actors, international organisations and transnational oil corporations. Central Asian states are particularly sensitive to security concerns. They still lack the experience that comes from independent statehood. They have not had the opportunity to develop a defined culture for strategic and security planning, or for policy engineering. Furthermore, these newly independent states tend to underestimate certain security threats, exaggerate others and sometimes even overlook vital factors in national security planning. Their strategic visions and calculations are mainly based on historical events with reference to ethnic lines.

Central Asia is an important region for India with its vital geo-strategic location. The five landlocked republics of Central Asia are in India's neighbourhood or extended neighbourhood. The region connects Asia with Europe. It occupies a special place in India's foreign policy priorities. Its importance to India today is not merely civilisational, but also linked to geo-political and economic issues. Central Asia has been of great significance to India in the past, and it remains so today as well. India's attempt has always been to increase political, cultural and economic ties with the Central Asian Republics (CARs).

Since 1991, India-CAR relations have come a long way. Although numerous political and economic changes have taken place in the recent past in these states, but the relationship between India and CARs has gone beyond the historical and cultural ties to a strong political and security cooperation. There are still significant common interests, on which India and CARs can accelerate future cooperation. India-CAR relations are aimed to counter common threats to their security, as both face the menace of terrorism. The struggle against terrorism is one major area of cooperation. Both, CARs and India share the view that the problem of drug trafficking and threat of weapons of mass destruction (WMD) are to be addressed jointly. On the situation in Afghanistan, both hold similar views. India and the CARs have signed a number of agreements to improve their relationship and cooperate in economic and energy sectors. Both have similar approaches towards major international and regional issues. There have been emergences of new strategic equation and security realignments in the region. Although India is not a key player in the region, these changes provide India both, opportunities as well as challenges in the region. After the events of September 11, 2001, India has also started building military technical cooperation with this region. India is also engaged with CARs in intelligence sharing, sharing of joint military experience and providing training and assistance to Central Asian forces.

Both India and Central Asia have economic complementarities in terms of resources, human resources and markets; which if exploited, can broaden cooperation. Opportunities for joint ventures in banking, insurance, agriculture, IT and pharmaceuticals also exist. The Indian pharmaceutical industry has done well in the CARs. Today, it accounts for nearly a quarter of the imports into the region. Indian industrialists have also registered an impressive presence in the steel and construction sectors. Given the policy preferences of the governments in the region, India would do well to lay emphasis on expanding its manufacturing and industrial activities in the CARs.

India is trying to exploit its expertise in the construction of small and medium-sized hydroelectric plants, mainly in Kyrgyzstan and Tajikistan, which have substantial hydropower potential. Also, with Central Asian energy reserves being estimated at 2.7% of world oil reserves (between 13 and 15 billion barrels) and 7% of natural gas reserves (around 270 to 360 trillion cubic feet, mainly in two big fields Kashag and Tangis), the region has potential as a future energy source for India. The main hydrocarbon deposits in the CARs are in Kazakhstan, Turkmenistan and Uzbekistan. The Central Asian states with energy potential (mainly Kazakhstan and Uzbekistan) are closely cooperating with India in the fields of oil and natural gas exploration and production. India and Uzbekistan have signed an agreement to conduct oil and gas exploration in Uzbekistan. Uzbekistan has also agreed to allocate geological territory to Indian companies to explore its hydrocarbon resources. The work is in progress between Gas Authority of India Ltd. (GAIL) and Uzbek-Neftogas to build facilities in Uzbekistan to produce LPG (liquefied petroleum gas). Forthcoming Turkmenistan-Afghanistan-Pakistan-India (TAPI) gas pipeline, will also transport the Caspian Sea's natural gas from Turkmenistan through Afghanistan into Pakistan and then to India. Turkmenistan will supply gas from its South Yoloten-Osman field. Oflate, Turkmenistan and India have also entered into a Gas Sales and Purchase Agreement (GSPA) with Turkmenistan's national oil firm called Turkmengaz.

In the field of defence, India had acquired six Ilyushin-78 in-flight re-fuelling aircraft from Uzbekistan. Indian aircrafts are being regularly serviced at the Chekalov aircraft plant in Tashkent. Uzbekistan has got the potential for intensifying cooperation between India and Uzbekistan in the aviation sector. Indian experts have been involved in repairing military aircraft in Tajikistan. Ayni Airbase in Tajikistan happens to be India's first and only foreign military base. Ayni, the Air Force base, is also known as Gissar Air Base. This is basically a military Air Base in Tajikistan, 10 kms west of the capital of Tajikistan, Dushanbe (used to be a major military base during the Soviet period). India's close relationship with Tajikistan helped India to create this Air Base there, even though it took almost 10 years for India after the disintegration of the Soviet Union to establish this strong connection with Tajikistan (India has spent almost $70 million between 2002 and 2010 to renovate the Ayni base). India has extended the Ayni runway to 3,200 meters and installed state-of-the-art navigational and air defence equipments there. India is interested in developing the Ayni Air Base project to gain a strategic foothold in Central Asia and improve its C3I (Command, Control, Communications and Intelligence) network, to strengthen its operations (mainly in Afghanistan). However, this base is still dormant without any fighter jets, and Tajik and Indian government have both ruled out any possibility of deployment of Indian forces at Ayniin January 2011. The importance of Tajikistan for India is significant, like other Central Asian states. Indians have become more ambitious and want to be involved more closely with Tajikistan and its people, and want to go beyond just running a hospital or maintaining an Air Base inside Tajikistan. Instead, India is now looking for bigger security role for itself in Tajikistan.

Apart from security issues, both India and Central Asia want to be part of an extended trade network through the North–South transport corridor. Science and technology is another area where India and CARs are now working together. India and the CARs, together, are now trying to develop the human resource potential in the region. India is in the process of building software development centres and light motor vehicles manufacturing sector in Central Asia. India's observer status in Shanghai Cooperation Organisation (SCO) has opened up further opportunities for cooperation with the CARs in areas like security, communication and economic integration, and it is expected that if India gets full membership in SCO, then this cooperation and partnerships will move even faster and better.

Prime Minister Narender Modi's recent visit to five Central Asian Republics (from 6th July till 13th July 2015) provided the much-needed impetus to the bilateral relationships. During this visit, PM Modi focused on the significant bilateral issues and concerns. The talks related to the energy cooperation (including gas, oil and Uranium), cooperation in counter-terrorism activities, in improving transport linkages, in defence cooperation (including training and exercises), were highlighted. This recent visit further enhanced cooperation in maintaining peace and stability and in ensuring regional security The overall outlook on the region suggests that for India, there is an enormous scope and potential to engage in meaningful and fruitful politico-economic cooperation with the CARs. Tourism, diplomacy, defence, education, food processing and products related to small-scale industries offer considerable potential for cooperation. The region could be used as a ground for joint ventures for producing goods and commodities for export to the wider world. Thus, India and CARs have both got immense potential to offer each other. However, there is still a need to look for ways to increase people-to-people contacts and step up information sharing. It is against this backdrop that all the chapters in this volume have tried to examine, and debate various aspects providing literary discourses and present dynamics of the region focusing on possible challenges. The chapter written by Dr. Halim Nezihoglu highlighted concerns related to the nation-building and national identity issues in post-Soviet Central Asia. Maj. Gen. Bal Krishan Sharma's chapter provided an in-depth analyses of terrorism in the Afghanistan-Pakistan (Af-Pak) region and its implications on regional security. Amb. Reena Pandey's chapter highlighted the positive trends in India-Kyrgyzstan bilateral relations, this chapter emphasised on the government-to-government contact between the two nations, and touched upon possible future cooperation. Dr. Ibrahim Konkak's chapter focuses on the external powers in Central Asia, while this chapter emphasises on the roles of major powers in shaping the external and internal policies of the Central Asian states. Dr. Nivedita Das Kundu's chapter dealt comprehensively with giving the overview of the role of great powers in Central Asia, discussing different perspective and focusing on general discourse on the topic. Dr. Raj Kumar's chapter on the Afghan factor in security of Central Asian Republics provided views on the security threats for the Central Asian states that emanate from Afghanistan. All the chapters in this volume touched upon various policy objectives, providing insight into the reality. The theme of the chapters dexterously worked out with well documented data. The chapters in this volume have got the potential to provide broad ideas to scholars, policy makers, academics in both India and Kyrgyzstan, and offer clarity on the significant topic under study.

REFERENCES

"India-Central Asia Economic Relations", Report of RIS/CII Seminar RIS-DP # 94/2005, May 2005.

Firdous T., "India and Central Asia", in M.A.Kaw and A.A. Banday eds. *Central Asia Introspection*, Crown Press, Srinagar, 2006, pp.321-322

Narula Kapil, "TAPI Pipeline Inching from Dream to Reality", available at https://www.indrastra.com/2015/12/FEATURED-TAPI-Pipeline-Inching-from-Dreams-to-Reality- by-Kapil-Narula-0513.html, accessed on 10th December 2015 "Regional-Economic-Cooperation-Creates-the-TAPI-Pipeline", available at http://www.economywatch.com/features/Regional-Economic-Cooperation-Creates-the-TAPI-Pipeline1204.html, accessed on 10th December 2015

Turkmen Foreign Ministry Report, August 2015.

"TAPI will meet Pakistan, India energy concerns", "The Statesman", 15th December 2015. "TAPI Project likely get start", "Deccan Herald", available at http://www.deccanherald.com/content/515890/tapi-project-likely-kick-start.html, accessed on 12th December 2015

Santhanam K, Baizakova K, Dwivedi R eds., "India-Kazakhstan Perspective", Anamaya Publishers, 2007

Santhanam K. Sultanov Bulat eds. "India-Kazakhstan Relations: Enhancing the Partnership", Anamaya Publishers, 2006 Kazakh-India Business, Issue 2, 2014 Kazakh Embassy Report, 2015

Santhanam K, Dwivedi R. eds., "India-Kyrgyz Relations: Perspective and Prospects", Anamaya Publishers 2006

"Faultline of Conflict in Central Asia and the South Caucasus", RAND Document, RAND Publications, 2003. Also see Kavalski, 2007, p. 854.

Kundu Das Nivedita, "Russia-India Strategic Ties : Indian Prime Minister's Visit to Russia", on 22nd December 2015, available at "Valdaiclub.com/news/russia-india-strategic-ties-indian-prime-minister-s-visit-to-russia/"

Kundu Das Nivedita, "Turkmenistan-Afghanistan-Pakistan-India (TAPI) Pipeline Project : From Dream to Reality", 16th December 2015, Valdai Publication http://valdaiclub.com/news/tapi-pipeline-project-from-dream-to-reality/

Kundu Das Nivedita, "TAPI: Ensures Regional Energy Security", "Strategic Perspective", United Service Institution of India, 16th December 2015, available at "http://usiofindia.org/Article/?pub=Strategic%20Perspective&pubno=46&ano=2826".

"Eurasian Journal of Business and Economics", Volume 7, Number 13, May 2014, available www.ejbe.org

Bibliography

A.L. Boyer, "Recreating the Silk Road: The Challenge of Overcoming Transaction Costs", *China and Eurasia Forum Quarterly*, Vol. 4, No. 4, 2006

Acharya Amitav and Johnston Alastair Iain, eds. "Crafting Cooperation: Regional International Institutions in Comparative Perspective", Cambridge University Press, Cambridge, 2007

Adler Emmanuel and Barnett Michael, eds., "Security Communities, Cambridge, Cambridge University Press, 1998

Alexander Lukin, ed., "Strategiya Rossii v Tsentralnoi Azii i Shankhayskoi organizatsii sotrudnichestva", Moscow, MGIMO, 2012

Allison Roy, "Virtual Regionalism, Regional Structures and Regime Security in Central Asia", *Central Asian Survey*, Vol. 27, No.2, 2008

Andrew Higgins, "In Central Asia, a new headache for U.S. policy", *Washington Post*, August, 31, 2010

Aris, Stephen, "Eurasian Regionalism e Shanghai Cooperation Organization", Basingstoke, Palgrave Macmillan, 2011

Dmitry Shlapentokh, "Turkey and Kyrgyzstan deepen ties", *CACI Analyst*, March 21, 2012

E. Vinokurov, M. Jadraliyev and Y. Shcherbanin, "The EurAsEC Transport Corridors: Sector Report", "Eurasian Development Bank", Almaty, March 2009

Faye M. L., Mcarthur J. W., Sachs J. D., Snow T., "The Challenges Facing Landlocked Developing Countries", *Journal of Human Development*, Vol. 5, No. 1, pp-31-66, March 2004

Fioramonti Lorenzo, ed., "Regions and Crises. New Challenges for Contemporary Regionalisms", Basingstoke, Palgrave Macmillan, 2012

Gulnoza Saidazimova, "Kyrgyzstan: Did Revolution Sow the Seeds of Democracy? (Part II), Prague, *RFE/RL,* April 8 2005

Gulnoza Saidazimova, "Kyrgyzstan: Youth Playing Key Role in Pro-Bakiyev Political Movement", (Part I) *RFE/RL,* July 7, 2005

H. Y. Malik, 'Strategic Importance of Gwadar Port', *Journal of Political Studies*, vol. 19th February, 2012

Idrissov E, "Great Gain, not Great Game, in Central Asia", *The Straits Times*, available at http://www.straitstimes.com/opinion/great-gain-not-great- game-in-central-asia

"Iran will help Kyrgyzstan go down the path of democracy: Larijani", *IRNA,* October 19,2011

Joshi, Nirmala, "Reconnecting India and Central Asia, Emerging Security and Economic Dimensions", Washington, D.C. 2010

K. Kumkova, "Kyrgyzstan & Tajikistan: Disputed Border Heightens Risk of Conflict", *Eurasia Net,* August 2, 2012

Kazharov Rustam, Nurova Nargis and Safranchuk Ivan, "Energeticheskoye sotrudnichestvo v ramkakh ShOS", Moscow, 2012

Koldunova Ekaterina, "Bezopasnost v Vostochnoi Azii: Novye vyzovy", Moscow, Navona, 2010

Kundu Das Nivedita, "12th SCO Summit in Beijing: A View from India", Valdai Discussion Club, available at http://valdaiclub.com/asia/44660.html

"Kyrgyzstan closes border crossing with Tajikistan", *Kyr TAg, Bishkek,* May 15, 2012.

Laruelle Marlene and Peyrouse Sébastien, 'Regionalnye organizatsii v Tsentralnoi Azii: kharakteristiki vzaimodeistviy, dilemmy e•ektivnosti', Report No.10, available at http://www.ucentralasia.org/downloads/UCA-IPPA-WP-10-RegionalOrganizations-Rus.pdf

Laruelle Marlene and Peyrouse Sébastien, "Chinese Question in Central Asia: Domestic Order, Social Change and the Chinese Factor", London, Hurst & Company, 2012

Lin Gang; Garver John; Hickey Dennis and Chambers Michael, "China's "Good Neighbor" Diplomacy: A Wolf in Sheep's Clothing?", "Asia Program Special Report", No. 126, 2005

Linn Johannes, 'Central Asian Regional Integration and Cooperation: Reality or Mirage?' EDB Eurasian Integration Yearbook 2012, Available at, URL http://www.brookings.edu/~/media/research/files/papers/2012/10/regional%20integration%20and%20cooperation%20linn/10%20regional%20integration%20and%20cooperation%20linn.pdf

Lukin Alexander, ed., "Strategiya Rossii v Tsentralnoi Azii i Shankhaiskoi organizatsii sotrudnichestva, Moscow, MGIMO, 2012

M. Emerson and E. Vinokurov, "Optimisation of Central Asian and Eurasian Trans-Continental Land Transport Corridors", EUCAM Working Paper no. 7, December 2009

Manmohan Parkash, "Connecting Central Asia: A Road Map for Regional Cooperation", ADB Manila, 2006

Mariya Y, Omelicheva Y. M., *Nationalism and Identity Construction in Central Asia: Dimensions, Dynamics, and Directions,* Lexington Books, 2014

"Obama administration lists Kyrgyzstan and Tajikistan as priority assistance countries in Central Asia for 2012", *AKIpress,* February 16, 2012

Olga Shumylo Tapiola, "The Eurasian Customs Union: Friend or Foe of the EU?" Carnegie Papers, Carnegie Endowment for International Peace, Brussels, October 2012

R. Pomfret, "Trade and Transport in Central Asia", "Emerging Markets Forum", Centennial Group report, Washington DC, January 2010

Richard Weitz, "Global Security Watch Russia: A Reference Handbook", *World Politics Review*, February 10, 2009

Rovshan Ibrahimov, "Azerbaijan Energy Strategy and the Importance of the Diversification of Exported Transport Routes", *Journal of Qafqaz University*, No 29, 2010

Rovshan Ibrahimov, "Azerbaijan`s Energy History and Policy: From Past till Our Days", in Rovshan Ibrahimov (ed.), "Energy and Azerbaijan: History, Strategy and Cooperation", SAM, Baku, 2013

S. Akiner ed., "The Caspian: Politics, Energy, Security", Routledge Curzon, London/NY, 2004

S. Akiner, "The Shanghai Cooperation Organisation: A Networking Organisation for a Networking World", Global Strategy Forum Paper, London, July 2010

S.F. Starr ed., "The New Silk Road: Transport and Trade in Greater Central Asia", Central Asia-Caucasus Institute Silk Road Studies Program, John Hopkins University-SAIS, Washington DC/ Uppsala University, Uppsala, 2007

Shumaila Andleeb, "Pakistan, Kyrgyzstan agree on reviving four-nation trade pact", APP, March 15, 2011

"Sovmestnoye zayavleniye po itogam ofitsialnogo visita v Respubliku Indiyu", Kremlin.ru, 2012

Starr Fedrric, "The New Central Asia", *YouTube*, available at https://www.youtube.com/watch?v=tIde2QSDwZk, Access date; January 16, 2016.

Walter Pincus, "Bethesda-based development firm gets Kyrgyzstan contract", *Washington Post*, October 24, 2010

Washington-based Silk Road Newline on February 15, 2012. Executive Budget Summary released by the Department of State said "The FY 2012 request prioritizes assistance for the Kyrgyz Republic to support the new Government's efforts to reform core institutions, law enforcement, and increase economic opportunities"

Zh. Zharmagambetova, L. Flake, "Kazakhstan: Grain and Feed Update", USDA Foreign Agricultural Service Global Agricultural Information Network (GAIN) Report, 25 July 2012,

Index